An Essay

on Christian Philosophy

Books by the Same Author

at
Philosophical Library, Inc.

The Dream of Descartes

The Philosophy of Nature

Art and Faith

Bergsonian Philosophy and Thomism

An Essay
on Christian Philosophy

by
Jacques Maritain

Translated by
Edward H. Flannery

PHILOSOPHICAL LIBRARY
NEW YORK

PRINTED IN THE UNITED STATES OF AMERICA
BY THE HADDON CRAFTSMEN, INC., SCRANTON, PA.

CONTENTS

Notes

TRANSLATOR'S FOREWORD

When the original version of *An Essay on Christian Philosophy* appeared in France, it was accepted in many quarters as the definitive statement of the Thomistic position on the subject. Some questions were raised, however, regarding certain theses upheld by Mr. Maritain in that study, and this led to further elucidations by him in another work, which was translated into English under the title *Science and Wisdom* (New York: Scribners). With the exception of the latter, the English reading public has never had access to a compact statement of Mr. Maritain's essential views on the nature and conditions of Christian philosophy. It is perhaps this fact more than any other which accounts for the fact that the fruitful debate on this important problem, which engaged the philosophers and theologians in Europe two decades ago, never quite managed to reach our own shores. It was in the interest of helping to reduce this "cultural lag" that the present translation was undertaken.

Although *An Essay on Christian Philosophy* is not ordinarily ranged among Maritain's greater works it is, in a sense, the key which unlocks the doors leading to the interior of his massive synthesis of modern Thomism, for it deals with the inner springs of his thought or, we might say, with his philosophical "founts of revelation." Its importance could not be better underlined than by this affirmation of Maritain himself: "The more I think about this problem of Christian philosophy the more it appears a central point of the history of our time since the Renaissance: and probably as the central point of the history of the age to come." (*Science and Wisdom,* p. 129)

Because of the purely philosophic nature of this study, the main effort in translation was for fidelity and clarity, at the cost, where necessary, of felicitous expression. For the sake of readers unacquainted with Scholastic thought I have appended a glossary of unfamiliar terms and phrases, which includes, for the most part, Scholastic or Latin terms or expressions which are undefined or untranslated when first encountered in the text. The lengthier Latin passages have also been rendered by the translator. And whenever Latin passages have appeared in the original text, they have, with the consent of the author, been relegated to footnotes and replaced by their English translation.

I wish to thank Mr. Maritain for reading the manuscript and for the corrections suggested. I should also like to express my thankfulness to Most Rev. Russell J. McVinney, D.D., of Providence, R. I., for his encouragement, and to Father John Oesterreicher of the Institute of Judaeo-Christian Studies of Seton Hall University for valuable suggestions.

E. H. F.

PREFACE

"Does a Christian philosophy exist? Is a Christian philosophy at all conceivable?" Speculative issues of the highest importance as to the nature of philosophy and the intellectual value of faith are involved in these questions, and the answers we shall give them should have a decisive practical bearing on certain basic spiritual attitudes. For the philosopher will shape his life and thinking in a particular way if he is of the opinion that to philosophize well he has to keep his philosophic labors apart from his life of prayer (supposing that he has one). And he will shape them in an entirely different way to the extent that he believes, contrariwise, that he ought to join them in an organic and living unity, and strive in his personal activities to have the *opus rationis* quickened and activated by this life of prayer, and by contemplative wisdom—while fully safeguarding its absolute rigor and special purity.

The same problem is encountered again, moreover, though in different terms, in the case of the artist, as also in the case of the historian or the exegete.

The following pages, which are wholly devoted to the problem of Christian philosophy, comprized the text of a conference delivered at the University of Louvain in December, 1931, wherein I took up anew and expanded a communication I had made to the

Société Française de Philosophie in March of the same year. The fact that a theologian of the stature of Father Garrigou-Lagrange and philosophers such as Étienne Gilson[1] and Gabriel Marcel saw fit to express their accord with the views I upheld on those occasions provided the necessary encouragement to have them published in their present form.

Two explanatory notes dealing with apologetics and the problem of moral philosophy adequately considered have been added as a supplement. I should like to call the attention of the specialists to the second of these. There in a style necessarily somewhat technical I have touched upon questions which affect the whole domain of practical knowledge and moral science. The answers they receive will be fraught with serious significance for the future of this science.

REFERENCE

1. In the second volume (p. 287-290) of his admirable book, *"L'Ésprit de la Philosophie Médiévale,"* Mr. Gilson, referring to this study, wrote: "Let me say that this account sets forth . . . the elements of a doctrinal solution to the problem. Not only do I believe that the historical point of view does not rule out the doctrinal one, but that it requires and, in a sense, implies it. In order that revelation may enlighten reason, both must form real mutual affinities in the subject in which they collaborate.

"Consider any given philosophic system. Now ask if it is 'Christian,' and if so by what characteristics you can recognize it as such? From the observer's standpoint it is a philosophy, therefore a work of reason. The author is a Christian, and yet his Christianity, however telling its influence on his philosophy has been, remains something essentially distinct from it. The only means at our disposal for de-

tecting this inner action is to compare the data which we can out-
wardly observe: the philosophy without revelation and the philosophy
with revelation. This is what I have attempted to do. And since
history alone is capable of performing this task, I have stated that
history alone can give a meaning to the concept of Christian philosophy. This conclusion will stand or fall with its premises. However,
should this formula or any other analogous that I have found of use
cause confusion, by reason of their very exactness, I am quite ready
to alter them.

"I may say, then, that Christian philosophy is an objectively
observable reality for history alone, and that its existence is positively
verifiable by history alone, but that once its existence has been
thus established its notion may be analysed in itself. This ought
to be done as Mr. J. Maritain has done it; I am in fact in complete
agreement with him. On the other hand, if Mr. Bréhier is right in
saying that Christian philosophy is not a historically observable
reality, or Mr. Blondel, that the Christian character of a philosophy
(supposing that it is possible) is in no wise indebted to revelation,
my position must be considered false."

An Essay

on Christian Philosophy

I

The Problem

1. There is a certain current of thought which tends to deny to human wisdom, to philosophy, an autonomous character in relation to religious faith. Originating in the far distant past,—we might say in the all-holy wisdom of Israel,—and assuming many widely diverse forms and shades, it has had its proponents in nearly every period of Christian history. According to it, philosophy, as a principle of truth, stands essentially in need of faith, or at least of some anticipation of or positive guidance toward the life of faith; and, moreover, any distinction between a purely natural wisdom and the wisdom of the Holy Spirit is akin to blasphemy. Some Russian orthodox thinkers, on the other hand, hold the opinion that the coming of faith to mankind has transformed philosophy in its very essence, and bestowed on it a new nature, new principles, and a new light all its own.

There is, on the contrary, another tradition which finds its inspiration in the Grecian Minerva. The rationalists—and even some neo-Thomists—infer that because philosophy is distinct from faith, it can have nothing in common with faith, save in an entirely extrinsic manner; so that the notion of Christian philosophy is not only complex in structure, but spurious, and unable to hold up under analysis. And there are many others who without giving open assent to this view indeed seem to develop their thought *as if* it were so.

What is most regrettable here is that both sides appear to be justified in their reproofs against their adversary. This, of course, is insufficient justification in an absolute sense; still it is enough to cause some perplexity at the very outset.

Recently Mr. Gilson gave a vigorous impetus to this debate, and set forth the question in its clearest terms.[1] In fact, he did more than simply pose the question; he contributed to it an invaluable historical elucidation in his work, *L'Esprit de la Philosophie Médiévale.*[2] Let me indicate straightway my basic agreement with him. However, whereas he has intentionally adopted the historical standpoint, I should like to attempt to bring together some elements of a solution on the doctrinal level.

The Rationalist Position

2. Another historian of philosophy, Mr. Émile Bréhier, has tried his hand at this same problem. His

study[3] is not wanting in interest or in vigor, and yet so simplified is its outlook that most of the time it is wide of the mark. In dread of "fixed" concepts and "ready made" things, and unwilling to know anything about philosophy and Christianity in themselves, the author seeks his answers from history. But in how fanciful a fashion! Indeed it is not history which replies that there is no Christian philosophy, and that "it is no more possible to speak of a Christian philosophy than of a Christian mathematics or physics." Even had all taken place just as he imagines (which I am certainly far from conceding), that is to say, if we had seen a series of attempts to construct a Christian philosophy founder one by one, from St. Augustine to Mr. Blondel, these attempts would not on that account have existed in a lesser degree or left a fainter impress on Western thought. Since when does history concede reality only to syntheses that have succeeded? For what systems are not in the end assimilated into something other than themselves? One philosophy alone boasts of greater durability, and it is precisely the value of this one that Mr. Bréhier is least inclined to acknowledge. It seems of late that rationalist dogmatism has introduced a new norm into the heart of history itself: the privilege of historical existence is to be reserved solely for whatever the historian's prejudices have approved as meritorious and sound.

But above all—and this deserves our particular attention—the means of differentiating employed by Mr.

Bréhier, as suitable as they may be for outlining some material traits, possess all too meagre a scope and accuracy for gauging the influence exerted on the domain of rational thought by a teaching and a way of life that transcend all philosophy.[4]

Furthermore, it would appear that despite his aversion toward "ready made" concepts, he himself conceives of religion as something alien in its very nature to intellectuality, and that this personal opinion has taken its toll of his entire handling of the question. Lastly, while he is right in noting that some of the systems which he reviews are Christian only in a material sense, his inquiry remains nevertheless unaccountably superficial when he comes to examine that philosophy which is usually regarded as the exemplar of Christian philosophy—I refer to medieval philosophy, and in an exceptional sense to the philosophy of St. Thomas Aquinas. The errors which can be singled out in his account are such that a Scholastic philosopher would certainly not be forgiven if he committed them in regard to a modern system. For example, St. Thomas definitely looked upon the human intellect as the weakest in the hierarchy of spirits; but never did he conceive of reason according to the merely dialectical and pathetically unstable pattern that Mr. Bréhier attributes to him; and never did he debar reason from "the possibility of being its own proper judge" (this does not mean its supreme judge). Never, yet again, did he reduce the relationship of reason and faith to that purely external "censorship," the workings of which Mr. Bréhier depicts with such naive abandon. (It is incontestable that for St. Thomas faith serves as a "negative norm" in relation to philosophy, yet this teaching does not bring us within the farthest flung outposts of the Thomistic teaching on faith and reason.) Never did he look on the multiplicity of individual intellects as a "miracle which is incompatible with the peculiar nature of intelligence";[5] never did he make individual differences consist of "accidents which spring from fleeting circumstance" . . .

Maurice Blondel's Solution

3. These pages were already written before the appearance of Mr. Maurice Blondel's book, *Le Probleme de la Philosophie Catholique,* in which he devotes a few chapters to Cardinal Dechamp's apologetical work.[6] Let me say at once that to the extent that Mr. Blondel affirms the value of Dechamp's apologetics he readily gains my assent.[7] The basic theme of this apologetics is, in my view, quite true, and I believe that it accounts for some primary realities, as well as for the common experience of souls. It can be fully squared, it seems to me, with the theological analyses of Fathers Gardeil[8] and Garrigou-Lagrange,[9] which are of such crucial importance, particularly so far as the essentially supernatural character of the formal motive of faith and the nature of apologetics itself[10] are concerned. Apolo-

getics, released from a particular academic rationalism, is thus genuinely restored, and at the same time enriched by an invaluable broadening of its speculative horizons and its practical methods. At most we might observe in regard to Dechamp's work (which, with good reason, remained more apostolic than systematic) that if the "method of Providence" actually excels the "method of the Schools," it is precisely on condition that it is allowed its full play. In my eye—a pessimistic eye—this method would be more endangered perhaps if it were taught in the Schools than if it were ignored by them. . . .

How could we fail to applaud Mr. Blondel's endeavors against the *separated* philosophy? Rightly he states that this conception of a *separated* philosophy is completely contrary to the spirit of Thomism. And truth to tell, the temptation which he denounced from his earliest works all too often finds free access to men's minds. (By this temptation—which Christians themselves breathe in with the atmosphere of the times—I understand that inclination to cut off reason in its own proper activities from higher sources of light, and, on the pretext that his object is purely natural, to look upon the philosopher himself as dwelling in a condition of pure nature; and again, on the pretext that his form of wisdom has no other inner criterion than reason alone, to see him as identified with Reason in itself, and as self-exempt from all need of natural or supernatural aids in the successful pursuit of his undertaking.)

In this light Mr. Blondel's philosophy assumes the proportions of a serious warning. It is with a certain melancholy that we find that truths which have been misunderstood and neglected in practice by so many have in the end wreaked their revenge by becoming embodied in a system in which the absence of keys to certain indispensable truths is all too keenly sensed. For in fine, no matter how many pains Mr. Blondel takes to clarify and refine his thought, one cannot forget that in his system of thought an insistence on our obligation not to separate or disconnect things from each other at times jeopardizes our corresponding obligation to make necessary distinctions between them. Despite the most conscientious attempts to discriminate, to reconcile differences, and to polish concepts he is still at great pains to transfer to the heart of a philosophy what holds true of an apologetics. (To achieve its purpose, apologetics, by its own nature and essence presupposes the solicitations of grace and the operations of the heart and will on the part of the one who hears, and the light of faith already possessed on the part of the one who speaks;[11] whereas philosophy by its nature and essence exacts neither faith as in the one nor the movements of grace and the heart as in the other, but only reason in the one who searches.)

There is, after all, a considerable difference between affirming the insufficiency of philosophy and constructing a philosophy of insufficiency. Mr. Blondel is convinced that if philosophy is to take cognizance of its limitations it must become cognizant also of the inadequacy of concepts and of "notional knowledge" for reaching reality. This amounts either to defining notional knowledge as using notions in a way that does violence to their nature, or else to disparaging the normal use of the proper instruments of intellectual cognition. Is it not highly remarkable, moreover, that in his last book Blondel should manifest so strong an aversion (in this he is almost at one with Mr. Bréhier) toward those who regard the inclusion of new, objective notions springing from the Judaeo-Christian revelation as one of the marks of Christian philosophy? This recognition of objective notions hitherto unknown or obscured by doubt, of truths which unaided reason is "physically" capable but "morally" incapable of grasping, and gathering together, in the purity of their meaning is not the only nor the chief attribute of Christian philosophy; but it is the most obvious and merits first consideration. And as true as it is that Christian concepts become lifeless forms wherever a Christian inspiration is lacking, they do not cease even as such to stay on as dead witnesses to a gift once received from above.

As a matter of fact, Mr. Blondel has misconstrued Mr. Gilson's[12] position on a number of points. His preference for dwelling on differences has prevented him from seeing that this position (which also is Mr. Jolivet's[13] and my own[14]) bids fair to do justice to an important part of his claims; I would say (and no doubt it is small comfort to be vindicated by a justification of this sort), to all that is valid in them. On the other hand, he doubtless had hardly counted on the surprizing shift on the part of those rationalists[15] who greeted, if not with definite favor at least with some sympathy, the conception of a philosophy which would be "catholic" (in its positive development and especially in its awareness of its own incompleteness) in so spontaneous a fashion that it would in no wise be beholden to revelation for "notional" data. Frankly, I find this conception chimerical from a historical standpoint, and for reasons expounded throughout this study doctrinally inadmissible.

II

Nature and State

4. In the light of Thomistic theory, then, what are we to think of the concept of Christian philosophy? Let me point out directly that in my opinion the principle of solution is to be found in the classical distinction between the *order of specification* and the *order of exercise,* or again, in the terminology which I shall adopt, between "nature" and "state." This means that we must distinguish between the *nature* of philosophy, or what it is in itself, and the *state* in which it exists in real fact, historically, in the human subject, and

which pertains to its concrete conditions of existence and exercise.

Such a distinction, evidently, takes it for granted that philosophy has a nature, and that it is *in itself* something well determined.

Now it is by means of an abstraction that we are able to reflect on the nature of philosophy in itself. This abstraction is not a mere fiction. Nor is it what the ancients termed *abstractio totalis,* that abstraction of the genus from the species, of the logical whole from its parts, which, as they very well knew, is prescientific. It is what they called *abstractio formalis,* that is, the drawing out of what is intelligible in reality, or of the complex of formal notes from the things which are, as it were, their bearers. This *abstractio formalis* is, to my mind, at the base of all scientific work. Thanks to it the mathematician is able to speak of ensembles, the metaphysician, of consciousness and mind; and thanks to it we are here able to speak of philosophy. Turning our gaze from existential conditions it lifts it to the order of essences; it posits a possible before our thought; in sum, it disregards the *state* to ponder the *nature*.

This distinction between *nature* and *state* is not of much consequence for the sciences. (Here I use science in the narrower sense of the word, that is to say, in so far as "science" is distinct from wisdom.) In point of fact, where science is concerned, human thought has not to do with any basically differing states, save those of culture and unculture; and the changing conditions of history have no more than an outward and accidental bearing on scientific work. We may of course speak of "Greek mathematics" or "Hindu logic," yet these designations are in the end wholly material.

The order of wisdom, in which I believe we must class philosophy, is quite another matter. For in the case of wisdom which, if we are to believe Aristotle, is a form of knowledge more divine than human, and which due to the weakness of our nature, "in so many respects enslaved," we hold with a tenuous grasp—in the case of wisdom, I say, the human mind experiences fundamentally differing states.

The Nature of Philosophy

5. In the teaching of St. Thomas, substances are specified absolutely and by virtue of themselves; their powers of operation, by virtue of their acts; and these latter, by virtue of their objects. If a particular development and dynamic organization of the spirit, which we know as philosophy, takes form in us, it will be —as in the case of every act of knowing, searching and judging—essentially related to an object to which it makes our intelligence adapted and co-natured; and it will be exclusively specified by this object. Hence it is uniquely in function of the object that philosophy is specified, and it is the object toward which it tends by virtue of itself (by no means the subject in which it resides) that determines its *nature*.

Within the realm of the real, created and uncreated, there exists a whole class of objects which are *of their nature attainable* through the natural faculties of the human mind. If this were not the case, the distinction between the natural and the supernatural, between the orders of grace and nature, would be illusory.

Thus, whether the form of knowledge which of itself is directed to the understanding of this universe of naturally attainable objects is actually achieved in human minds or not, and even if it is achieved with more or less serious deficiencies and flaws, its essence is clearly marked out: it is intrinsically a natural and rational form of knowledge.

St. Thomas, it is true, was satisfied with a less arrogant idea of reason than Descartes or Spinoza. And yet, it was in a fully and integrally rational sense, though surely not in a rationalist one, that he looked on philosophic wisdom as the perfect achievement of reason, *perfectum opus rationis*.[16]

Whoever fails to recognize that the philosophic domain is of its nature within the reach of the sole natural faculties of the human mind—whatever else his conception of philosophy may embrace—negates philosophy; he does not define it.

The affirmation of this *natural* or *rational* character of philosophy is basic with St. Thomas. It may be said that by the very fact that he is a Christian it takes on an added value and import compared with the views of an Aristotle, who had no idea of an order of revelation. Such an affirmation, as made precise and explicit in relation to knowledge obtained through faith and theology—from which it sharply differentiates philosophy—ought to be valued as a definitive acquisition gained during the "progress of Western consciousness." If we are reluctant to forfeit it at any price, it is in order to safeguard the exact nature of faith and reason and remain true to essences, and to keep intact the primordial distinction between the natural and supernatural orders. Viewed as a formally constructed philosophy, Thomistic philosophy—I do not say Thomistic theology—is wholly rational: no reasoning issuing from faith finds its way into its inner fabric; it derives intrinsically from reason and rational criticism alone; and its soundness as a philosophy is based entirely on experimental or intellectual evidence and on logical proof.

From these considerations it follows that since the specification of philosophy hinges entirely on its formal object, and since this object is wholly of the rational order, philosophy considered in itself—whether in a pagan or Christian mind—depends on the same strictly natural or rational intrinsic criteria. So that the designation *Christian* which we apply to a philosophy does not refer to that which constitutes it in its *philosophic essence:* simply as a philosophy, *reduplicative ut sic,* it is independent of the Christian faith as to its object, its principles, and its methods.

Let us not be unmindful, however, that we are

dealing here with a pure, abstract essence. It is all too easy a matter to endow such an abstraction with reality, to clothe it as such with a concrete existence. An ideological monster results; such as, in my opinion, occurred in the case both of the rationalists, and the neo-Thomists whom Mr. Gilson has called to task.

History seems to indicate that at the time of Guillaume de Vair and of Charron, and later of Descartes, certain thinkers, who still professed the Christian faith, conjured up a man of pure nature whose lot it was to philosophize, and to whom might be superadded a man of the theological virtues destined to merit heaven. Later on the non-Christian rationalists, more logical in the same error, were to slough off this man of the theological virtues as a superfluous counterpart; they satisfied themselves that to philosophize properly, that is to say, according to the exigencies of reason, it is necessary to believe only in reason, in other words to be only a philosopher, existing only *qua* philosopher. What they failed to see was that in so doing they made of the philosopher a simple *hypostasierung* of philosophy, and denied him existence as a man, asking him to lose his soul for the sake of his object. But where man departs philosophy can no longer remain.

III

The Christian State of Philosophy

6. As soon as it no longer is a question of philosophy considered in itself but of the manner in which men philosophize, and of the divers philosophies which the concrete course of history has brought into existence, the consideration of the *essence* of philosophy no longer suffices; that of its *state* must be undertaken.

From this viewpoint of the state, or the conditions of exercise, it is manifest that before philosophy can attain its full, normal development in the mind it will exact of the individual many emendations and purifications, a disciplining not only of the reason but of the heart as well. To philosophize man must put his whole soul into play, in much the same manner that to run he must use his heart and lungs.

And here we encounter what in my opinion is the crucial point of the discussion, a point, moreover, at which dissent among Christians and non-Christians becomes unavoidable. One does not have to be a Christian to be convinced that our nature is weak (although the Christian's knowledge that nature is wounded makes him more keenly aware of these matters), or that the mere fact that wisdom is an arduous attainment is enough to account for the very high incidence of error in this area. But the Christian believes that grace changes man's state by elevating his nature to the supernatural plane and by divulging to him things which unaided reason would be unable to grasp. He also believes that if reason is to attain without admixture of error the highest truths that are naturally within its ken it requires assistance, either from within in the form of inner strengthening or from without in the form of an offering of objective data; and he believes that such assistance has in fact become so much an established part of things under the New Law that it has ushered in a new regimen for human intelligence.

This regimen directly involves functions higher than philosophy; nevertheless, with Mr. Gilson, I think that its results are written in the pages of the history of philosophy itself. It is also my view that purely rational norms empower us to pass a value-judgment on these philosophic results. Be that as it may, I should like for the moment to outline briefly what to my mind are the chief components of this *Christian state* of philosophy.

Objective Contributions

7. First and foremost, there are those data which by their nature belong within the field of philosophy, but which in actual fact philosophers failed to recognize explicitly, and which were placed in front rank by Christian revelation. Take for example the idea of *creation*. Here also belongs the idea of a *nature* which,

albeit real and intrinsically consistent (this the Hindus failed to see), is not an absolute closed upon itself, and is capable (this the Greeks did not see) of being perfected by a supernatural order. Or again, to take up one of Mr. Gilson's themes, there is the idea of God as *Subsisting Being Itself:* an idea which was set down by Moses, scarcely surmised by Aristotle (did he not call God ἡ ἀρχὴ καὶ τὸ πρῶτον τῶν ὄντων?[17] though his main interest lay elsewhere), and which the Christian Doctors drew from Aristotle thanks to Moses. Then, in the moral sphere, we have the idea of *sin,* in the fully ethical sense of an offense against God, an idea of which in spite of manifold attempts Western philosophy has not managed to rid itself.

Ideas of this kind are of paramount importance for the whole of philosophy. And in the case of each, reason has unquestionably received a positive endowment from revelation, so that we may again join Mr. Gilson to speak of *revelation begetting reason.* But on this point, it seems to me, a few distinctions are in order.

Interpreted in its fullest sense, this expression would apply to theology, which bears on the entire revealed datum and studies it from the standpoint of God, its Source. When applied to philosophy, the word revelation should not be deemed to refer to the whole revealed deposit but simply to those elements of the natural order that are contained therein or related thereto. The moment philosophy is advised of these elements, it scrutinizes them according to its own order, which *ascends* from experience toward things divine (whereas revelation *descends* from God).

And yet, by the very fact that the data under discussion naturally belong in the rational or philosophic realm, should they not have been implicated in some way, even the most virtual, in the philosophic treasury of mankind; so that we may not say that prior to revelation they were *totally* overlooked by the philosophers? Surely it is not in terms like these that the question ought to be raised. For as a general rule, and even in the case (which is not that of the notions which concern us here) of essentially supernatural revealed truths, the sudden appearance of absolutely original concepts (and nomenclature) is not required—which holds true even when the truths to be expressed are absolutely new to reason. (Were they absolutely original, no one would comprehend them. God acts reasonably: that is a hypothesis which the critics who busy themselves with the "sources" of dogma might well entertain. In order, for example, that the essentially supraphilosophic notion of the consubstantial *Logos* might be imparted to mankind in useful form, there was needed—the Christian outlook itself demands it—a conceptual preparation and a prolonged philosophic concern with the idea of a *logos*. Thus *logos,* both as an idea and a term, was ready at hand to prepare on the side of "material causality" the conditions requisite for the revelation of the Son. In this revelation, however, we did not have the *same* idea of the *logos,* the revealed idea; the idea of *logos* differed essentially from the philosophic one,[18] and thus was manifest on the side of "formal causality" the transcendence of the revelation of the Son.)

But let us get back to our discussion of the revealed truths of the natural order and the nescience of the early philosophers relative to the profoundest and loftiest of them. We were in the course of saying that this nescience was less a sheer and total night than a twilight more or less shadowy wherein thought is brought to a standstill or goes astray. In short, the question at issue here is rather concerned—and this is still of paramount factual importance—with differences of clarity that are, to tell the truth, extraordinarily pronounced: what used to dwell in regions of shadow or mirage is brought forth in the full light of day. Concomitantly, with the center of irradiation thus displaced, and with regions which our naturally weak eyes find obscurest now sending forth a most vivid brightness, everything takes on a fresh hue, and every view is transfigured.

8. We come across another class of objective data which philosophy knew well but which it approached with much hesitancy, and which, though not a part of revelation, was corroborated by revelation. In the noetic order, for instance, the Christian sees the validity of reason divinely confirmed—recall St. Augustine's controversies with the Academicians—by the fact that the

act of faith, notwithstanding its supra-rational character, is eminently reasonable. In this confirmation of the
validity of reason he sees by implication the validity
of many certitudes of the rational sphere which relate
to discerning the motives of credibility.

9. Finally, the fortunes of philosophy are involved
both by right and in fact, with that very portion of
the revealed deposit which no longer has to do with
data rational in their nature but with essentially supernatural mysteries.

This is so, first of all, because in a Christian regime
of thought philosophy is used by theology as an instrumental organ in the effort to elucidate these mysteries;
how could it possibly not learn many things while being
thus led along paths which are not its own?

Secondly, even when it keeps on working on its own
account, its field of inquiry is thereupon considerably
broadened. Philosophy seeks enlightenment about sensible objects from the natural sciences; what is to
prevent it from learning of divine things from faith
and theology? "The facts of religion or the established
dogmas are objects of my experience," Malebranche
declared,—once they have been brought to my attention, "I employ my mind in the selfsame manner as
the student of Physics"; and hereby he shared in the
very movement of Christian thought—this despite the
fact that on another level he had made the mistake of
lumping together philosophy and theology, and of

failing to appreciate that philosophy is powerless to make its abode in a zone of experience which surpasses it. It has often been remarked that unless there had been speculation on the dogmas of the Trinity and the Incarnation, it is exceedingly unlikely that the philosophers would have come to an awareness of the metaphysical problem of the person.

This is not all. The philosopher's experience itself has been revitalized by Christianity. He is offered as a *datum* a world that is the handiwork of the Word, wherein everything bespeaks the Infinite Spirit to finite spirits who know themselves as spirits. What a starting point! Here is, as it were, a fraternal attitude towards things and reality,—I mean in so far as they are *knowable*—for which the progress of the human mind is indebted to the Christian Middle Ages. There is every indication that it was this attitude which laid the groundwork for the flowering of the empirical sciences on the one hand and for the expansion of reflective knowledge in which modern times pride themselves on the other.

We should do well, finally, to pay attention, with Mr. Gabriel Marcel, to the paradox, the scandal if you wish, confronting reason which resides in the very fact that the quality of the revealed datum absolutely transcends all and every experience that can be constructed on purely human bases. It would seem, then, that there can be no genuinely Christian philosophy "except where this paradox, this scandal, is not merely admitted, or even accepted, but *embraced* with fervid gratitude and without qualification. As soon as the philosopher seeks, on the contrary, by any means whatsoever to tone down this scandal, disguise this paradox, or catch up the revealed datum in a dialectic of reason or of pure mind, he ceases to that precise extent to be a Christian philosopher." . . . We might say in this same vein that a Christian philosophy "discovers its ontological pivotal center" outside and above the entire philosophic order "in that fact, *unique* and beyond all compare, which is the Incarnation." And it does not seem exaggerated to assume that in the firmament of the soul the vital impulse which energizes a like philosophy from above consists in a "meditation on all the various implications and consequences of this datum, which is not only unforeseeable but contrary to certain superficial claims of reason which in first instance are wrongly presumed to be unimpeachable." Metaphysical reflection, thus restored to its own authentic natural spirituality, will then proceed to test these claims "in the name of higher claims"—in the name of claims of a reason which is genuinely pure and "which, moreover, faith in the Incarnation renders capable of achieving full self awareness. . . ."[19]

Subjective Aids

10. The preceding observation brings up another consideration, namely, the subjective reinforcement

which Christian philosophy is heir to in a Christian climate. First, so far as the formation, not yet the exercise, of the philosophic *habitus* in the mind is concerned, we may note that those natural convictions of reason, which I am loath to call common sense (since this expression is equivocal; and there is in fact a certain school of ethnology which is anything but helpful in working out the critical analysis which it needs today more than ever)—we may note, I say, that that which constitutes the truly natural in common sense serves as spiritual matrix, so to speak, in the shaping of intellectual states or capacities *(habitus)*. But, this natural reason itself is corroborated by religion. It is religion after all which places us in a coherent universe made up of things and persons with clearly defined natures, a universe wherein we must elect between a yes and no.

Relying on Mr. Piaget's tests, Mr. Léon Brunschvicg recently suggested that the Scholastic mentality is on the level of childhood—of children from eight to eleven years of age, if I am not mistaken (for these tests furnish thoroughly particularized answers—that is, of course, with respect to only one term of the comparison). This assertion might well be described as rash, and rich to boot in mistakes (and to say the least, such as makes a reply in kind all too easy, for to the charge that "the thinking preceding the XVII Century never reached maturity," what is to prevent the equally gratuitous retort that that following the XVII Century is *over-*

mature or senile?). And yet in another sense I find his appraisal quite gratifying. Happy indeed is the philosophy which has not lost touch with childhood, and which preserves not the levity but the vitality thereof, as well as those primordial assurances fashioned in our souls from the first dawn of reason by the Word enlightening every man coming into this world. These assurances it will verify and judge, it will never forfeit them.

11. But let us discuss the workings of the mind in which philosophy has already taken root. Philosophy is a certain perfection of the intelligence. In the eyes of an Aristotle it was the uppermost; whereas in St. Thomas' view, philosophy being solely natural in itself, ranks below the spiritual organism composed of the theological virtues and the gifts of the Holy Spirit, and below theology, a rational discipline rooted in grace-given faith. (I am referring here to St. Thomas the theologian, as indeed I needs must if I am to have a complete idea of his position on the problem under discussion.) Now the higher virtues succor the lowlier in the proper sphere of the latter. The virtue of faith, for example, enables the philosopher, who knows of the existence of God by purely natural means to adhere rationally to this truth with a sturdier grasp. Or to take another example, the contemplative *habitus* clarifies and soothes, spiritualizes the philosophic *habitus* within its own order. And in the light of theology,

metaphysical truths take on a radiance so immediate and convincing that in consequence the philosopher's labors are blest with a new facility and fruitfulness. Henceforth, in fact, metaphysics cannot assume its fullest proportions in the human mind without experiencing the attraction of theology; any more than theology in turn can find its own therein without the attraction of infused wisdom. Thus, this synergy and vital solidarity, this dynamic continuity of *habitus,* according to the Thomists (who distinguish not in order to separate but to unite), confers on philosophic activity a subjective reinforcement and refining of capital importance.

Other aids of a subjective nature stem from the order of finality. To be a prince or merely his minister is not an alternative which affects a man's nature, but it considerably alters his state. In one sense, the advent of Christianity did dethrone philosophic wisdom and raise theological wisdom and the wisdom of the Holy Spirit above it. Once philosophy acknowledges this new arrangement, its condition in the human mind is thoroughly changed. I think that every great philosophy harbors a mystical yearning, which in fact is quite capable of throwing it out of joint. In a Christian regime, philosophy understands that even if it can and ought to sharpen this desire, it is not up to philosophy itself to consummate it. Philosophy, then, is wholly orientated toward a higher wisdom, and thus it is made able to achieve some degree of self-detachment and be relieved of some of its ponderousness.

Lastly, as I recalled earlier, man's nature was wounded by original sin; and although these wounds for the most part involve the sphere of our love and our relationship to the last end and the distress brought by our unruly appetites, nevertheless it is perhaps in the domain of speculative thought more than anywhere else that this disorder and the obstacles it creates inflict damages that are most shocking from the point of view of the mind. But, grace produces more than its strictly supernatural effects in us: the divine life which it engrafts in our souls is endowed with a healing power with respect to our nature. Though permanently wounded, nature is henceforth convalescing, for it suffers a second wound, bearing on itself the all-pure wounds of the Savior, which transpierce the corrupt wounds of the old Adam. It would be absurd to expect the *gratia sanans* to supply for the philosophic *habitus,* or to preclude aberrations, even to the gravest kind. Yet it is certain that the more the philosopher remains faithful to grace, the more easily will he free himself of manifold futilities and opacities, which are as a mote of self-love on the eye of reason.

In sum, we understand that the state of philosophy has been changed and lifted up by Christianity, not only with respect to the objective material proposed but also with respect to the vitality and deepest dynamism of the intellect. On all these counts it must be affirmed that faith guides or orientates philosophy, *veluti stella rectrix,* without thereby violating its autonomy; for it is always in keeping with its own proper laws and principles and by virtue of rational norms alone that philosophy judges things. This is true even of those things which, albeit naturally accessible to reason alone, would not in reality be recognized or preserved by reason without taint of error, if reason had not been at once notified of their existence and fortified in itself through a kind of living continuity with superior lights.

Conclusions

12. These explanations, which touch on concrete relationships that extend indefinitely, could be carried to considerable length. Reducing them to essentials, however, I have held to a simple outline, my sole purpose being to work out in more precise detail the meaning of the distinction I have made between philosophy considered in its *nature* and philosophy considered in its *state* in the human mind.

We see now how the expression Christian philosophy does not designate a simple essence but a complex, that is, an essence taken in a particular state. Whence some unavoidable want of precision surrounding this expression, which for that matter stands for something very real. Christian philosophy is not a determinate body of truths, although, in my opinion, the doctrine

of St. Thomas exemplifies its amplest and purest form.
Christian philosophy is philosophy itself in so far as
it is situated in those utterly distinctive conditions of
existence and exercise into which Christianity has
ushered the thinking subject, and as a result of which
philosophy *perceives* certain objects and *validly demon-
strates* certain propositions, which in any other circum-
stances would to a greater or lesser extent elude it.
This is, therefore, entirely an interior qualification,
which informs and molds the determining marks of a
particular doctrinal *family*. Thus once more do we
arrive at Mr. Gilson's conclusions: "Though their relationship is intrinsic, the two orders remain distinct."
This relationship is not an accidental one: it results
from the very nature of philosophy, from its natural
longing to know its proper objects as well as possible,
as also from the very nature of the Christian doctrine
and life, and from the inner and outer bolstering which
they afford reason. So far as Thomism in particular is
concerned, first we must say that if it is a philosophy
at all, it is so to the point that it is rational, not to the
point that it is Christian. For another thing, if we
take the viewpoint, not of formal causality, but of
historical development, it must be admitted that Thomism owes its standing as a true philosophy not only
to reason but also to the sustenance it receives from
above, from that which, according to the Eudemian
Ethics, being the source of reason, is greater than
reason. The fact remains that what counts in a philos-

ophy is not that it is Christian but that it is true. I reiterate, no matter what the conditions of its development and its exercise in the soul may be, philosophy depends on reason; and the truer it is, the more will it remain rigorously faithful—and if I may say so, fastened—to its philosophic nature. It is for this reason that far from being shocked, as are some, by the fact that St. Thomas Aquinas procured his philosophical armour from the soundest thinker of pagan antiquity, I find therein a real source of intellectual stimulation.

13. In view of this, it is evident that a philosophy can be Christian and yet to a greater or lesser degree fall short of the requirements of its philosophic nature. When this happens, we have less to deal with Christian philosophy than with its decadence or disintegration; an instance of which was seen in the days when Occamism held sway in the Universities.

Thus we are led to distinguish between what we may call an organic Christian regime, such as human intelligence knew (not without many a flaw) in the finest hour of medieval civilization, and a dissociated Christian regime, which it experienced during subsequent epochs. In point of fact, Western philosophy has never set itself free of Christianity: wherever Christianity did not have a hand in the construction of modern philosophy it served instead as a stumbling-block. In this context, Nicholas Berdyaev would say that all great modern philosophies (and even, to be sure, that of a Feuerbach) are "Christian" philosophies, philosophies which without Christianity would not be what they are.

Let us bear in mind that if we are to grasp Christian thought in its integrity we must take into account not only philosophy (even Christian) but also, and inseparably, theology and the wisdom of the contemplatives. Today as a consequence of the breakdown of Christian unity, philosophy has fallen heir to all kinds of tasks, preoccupations, and troubles which in former times were part and parcel of the other two forms of wisdom. (An example of this is seen in the idea of the Kingdom of God, which the philosophers turned into the Realm of Minds and finally into Mankind in the sense of a Herder or an Auguste Comte.) As philosophy became inwardly less Christian it grew fat on the leftovers of Christian consciousness. This accounts for the paradox of a philosophy like that of Descartes, or even of Hegel, appearing more deeply tinged with Christianity and less strictly philosophic than the formally Aristotelian (but inspirationally supra-Aristotelian) philosophy of St. Thomas Aquinas.

14. It is, as we have seen, on the twofold level of objective endowments and subjective strengthening that Christianity has acted upon the depths of philosophic thought. As a general rule, the effects of what

we have termed a dissociated Christian regime take the form of a disastrous disturbance of the balance normally required between these two levels, let us say between *object* and *inspiration*.

In one instance, a thinking which has turned its back on higher lights is still encumbered with Christian data, which have begun to crumble; no longer *living* in a body of thought consonant with their true meaning and drawing their inspiration from a brand of reason that has grown increasingly sluggish, they have become distorted and corrupt. So it is that at each decisive turning of modern rationalism we are able to detect a *materialization* of truths and notions of Christian origin.

In the second instance, quite the opposite occurs. Here a Christian inspiration, deprived of the objective norms and nutriments which it needs by nature, has run amok and lays waste the field of rational speculation. (The more grandiose this inspiration remains the more severe will its ravages be.) Though for differing reasons and in varying degrees, we should have to mention in this connection, a Böhme, a Jacobi, possibly a Schelling, a Kierkegaard, and a Nietzsche. I recognize full well that their achievement is replete with precious stimulations and constitutes a testimony of lofty significance; the claims of truth, however, compel me to state that it represents a corruption of philosophy as such. Its uncommonly violent tastes can be traced to this very fact.

IV

Theology and Philosophy

15. Before completing these pages I should like to propose a few further remarks. First of all, a few words about the relations of theology and philosophy. In my opinion, many an account of medieval philosophy has been impaired or vitiated by an insufficiently drawn distinction between these two disciplines.

Some seem to think that theology supplies cut and dried answers to the major philosophic questions, and in this way nullifies the endeavors of philosophy. Then there are those who fancy that in a Christian regime philosophy is subjugated to theology.

In real fact, theology possesses an object, a light, and a method that differ entirely from those of philosophy. Rooted in faith, it conducts its reasoning on the authority of the revealed word and proceeds *ex causa prima;* its object is the revealed datum itself, which it seeks to elucidate rationally.[20]

When, therefore, a particular theological inquiry happens to provide an answer to a philosophic question, this answer is not given *philosophically;* the whole philosophic endeavor is to move along another plane. Philosophy, moreover, is not paralyzed but rather stimulated by this state of affairs. In fact, the mighty intellectual curiosity which stirred the Christian ages can only be explained against the background of the sublime mysteries propounded to them.

A word about the adage *philosophia ancilla theologiae*. Its origin, of course, is to be sought in St. Peter Damiani, who intended to silence philosophy with it. The Scholastic position is something entirely different. Therein philosophy is placed in the service of theology when, and only when, in its own workings theology employs philosophy as an *instrument* of truth in order to establish conclusions which are not philosophic but theological. *Ancilla*, then, it may be, but not *serva*, for theology handles philosophy in accordance with its own proper laws; a Minister of state yes, but a slave it can never be.

But in itself, or when engaged in its own pursuits, philosophy is not a handmaid; it is free, it enjoys the freedom to which as a form of wisdom it is entitled. I am fully aware that revelation *teaches* it certain truths, including philosophic. Even so, God alone is not subject to being taught, the angels themselves enlighten one another; being taught does not stifle the freedom of the mind, but merely attests that it is a created freedom. And for every created spirit truth holds primacy even over the quest for knowledge, however noble this quest may be. Some modern philosophers who disbelieve in Christian revelation presume to judge in terms of their own peculiar assumptions concerning this revelation the relationship established in the Christian system between philosophy and faith. Their method leaves something to be desired, for their assumptions are without validity save in a non-Christian system. Surely, if I did not believe that the primordial Truth itself is my teacher in the tenets of faith, if I believed that faith presents me with a mere code binding me to a human tradition, I would not accept the subordination of philosophy to faith. What I mean to say, in fine, is that no one will grant that philosophy should suffer duress: neither the non-Christian, in whose eyes faith would impose restraints on philosophy and obstruct its view; nor the Christian, for whom faith does not restrain philosophy but strengthens it and helps it to improve its vision.

And yet, as in the case of every organic regime, certain drawbacks more or less serious in nature can accidentally *(per accidens)* spring from the vital solidarity established in a Christian regime among the hierarchically ordered virtues of the intellect. Thus, in the Middle Ages philosophic problems, while being stirred up by theology, often remained posed too exclusively in function of theology. Thomistic philosophy suffered some impairment of a secondary sort in this respect; not as to its innermost worth, to be sure, but as to the autonomy of its organization. One of the causes of misunderstanding which estrange "scholastics" and "moderns" today, I believe, rests on the fact that exactly those very enrichments—the admirable purity and profundity—which this philosophy owes to its enlistment in the service of theology and to its captivation by a superior light, have slowed down its technical elaboration in an autonomous doctrinal body, wherein it would lead a life of its own outside the theological organism and proceed in all its parts and without exception according to the due methods and modes of philosophy. Let me say here that Thomistic philosophy, completely distinct in itself from theology, and dwelling, as it always must, both in its own home and in that theology (where it is *better off* than in its own), has still many tasks, arrangements, and re-classification of materials to attend to before it can finally take up residence in its own quarters—without breaking off its vital relations with theology in the process. Even though these quarters cannot boast of the spacious chambers and lofty ceilings of theology's imposing mansion, it has withal the duty not to neglect them.

Yet it is my belief that these drawbacks which origi-nated in a regime of openly declared subordination were of a less serious nature than those brought about by the subordination of philosophy to undeclared theologies and mystical urges.

At any rate, it is not solely to Plato, but far more— and in fact by a much closer historical bond—to the theologians and philosophers of the Middle Ages that the modern Western world is indebted for the very concept of a purely objective science, and for all the intellectual self discipline that it entails. This puri-fication of the speculative is one of the attainments of Christian philosophy.

Finally, as we observed earlier, distinction does

not mean separation. Once the distinction between the respective natures of philosophy and theology is acknowledged, there is nothing to forbid thought, now equipped in both disciplines, to pass in a single, concrete movement from one to the other. What theory sunders is at one in life. A free Christian wisdom which unites the philosophic and theological lights without confusing them, can accordingly follow out a line of thought which resembles, if you wish, that of Malebranche—without mixing up formal objects as he does, however.

Moral Philosophy Adequately Considered

16. We should do well to dwell here in a very special way on the peculiar characteristics of those problems which concern the human person. In so far as they deal with the purely speculative study, whether metaphysical or psychological, of the psycho-physical functions and spiritual faculties of the human composite they involve no other difficulty than any other philosophic problem. But when we take as our object human action,—that universe of man and human things envisaged in their moral dynamism and in relation to their proper end—our considerations take an entirely new turn, in fact, a practical one. Here the case assumes a very special character. For we are face to face with an object which itself presents us with distinction between *nature* and *state:* an object which

is *natural* by virtue of its essence, but whose *state* is not purely natural, and depends on the supernatural order.

Man is not in a state of pure nature, he is fallen and redeemed. Consequently, ethics, in the widest sense of the word, that is, in so far as it bears on all matters of human action, politics and economics, practical psychology, collective psychology, sociology, as well as individual morality,—ethics in so far as it takes man in his concrete state, in his existential being, is not a purely philosophic discipline. Of itself it has to do with theology, either to become integrated with or at least subalternated to theology.

It is here that the combining of philosophic and theological lights which I mentioned a while ago acquires an exceptional importance. For one thing, theology, proceeding in conformity with its own proper mode, *ex prima causa,* and on the authority of the revealed word, encompasses this practical realm in its all-embracing wisdom. In virtue of its higher unity it is, as we know, in a formal and supreme manner, both a speculative and a practical science.

Then again, the philosopher cannot possibly refrain from scrutinizing, from his own peculiar standpoint and with his own tools, these same problems, and from entering into this universe of the specifically human— nay more, even into the world of spirituality, grace, and holiness, because this world is at the heart of the universe of man *existentially* considered.[21] And thus are we brought face to face with a philosophy that is Christian in a pre-eminent and altogether strict sense: a philosophy which *cannot* be proportioned to its object unless it makes use of principles received from faith and theology, and is enlightened by these latter. Here is a practical philosophy which remains a philosophy and proceeds according to the proper mode of philosophy, yet which is not purely and simply a philosophy. Here is a philosophy which must of necessity be a superelevated philosophy, a philosophy subalternated to theology,[22] if it is not to misrepresent and scientifically distort its object. What can happen in this latter respect is readily observable in our own day in the works of so many psychologists, psychiatrists, neurologists, pedagogues, sociologists, or anthropologists, whenever they deal with religious and mystical phenomena,—or even with the humblest ethical phenomena, or again even with psychotic and neurotic phenomena,—with which the human being provides them at his own expense.

It is well worth our while thus to disengage the idea of an authentic philosophy of human things. It is, I think, of no small interest for us clearly to recognize the true place of this practical philosophy adequately considered, or taken in its fullest sense, which is Christian by reason of the very characteristics of its object and in which the lights of reason and faith, of philosophy and theology are inter-connected; and to recognize that it has yet many discoveries to make. When it has won a larger measure of self-awareness it will appreciate the vast field that lies before it.

From the epistemological viewpoint, philosophy here no longer appears as taken up as an instrument by theology, but as subordinating itself thereto for the purpose of exploring a domain which is not all its own. Thanks, moreover, to the supplemental light and knowledge thus received, it is able to go forward in accord with the method proper to it, proceeding *ex propriis rerum causis* and rationally elucidating experience. The domain we are discussing is common to theology and to this practical philosophy adequately considered. This latter, however, studies it in a way and from a viewpoint all its own: by virtue of its very nature as a human form of knowledge it is called upon while working therein to give itself over to a more particularized kind of research, in which induction, hypothesis, and probability will be accorded a much more prominent role. Theology, in contrast, cannot come to any conclusion without recourse to the revealed datum. In the latter case, faith appeals to reason, as it would to a servant and friend, to help it to unfold its own divine treasures; in the other, we have reason calling upon faith, as upon a divine friend, for help in discovering among its earthly treasures certain riches which a supra-terrestrial alloy has made either too heavy or too mercurial for its own hands.

17. Metaphysics itself happens to be interested, albeit somewhat indirectly, in such a practical philosophy. For man is part of the universe, and the world of human action is intrinsically linked to the great universe of

creation. Besides, if reason left all to itself is able to stammer some very general and indefinite truths concerning the problems of evil and of divine governance, for example, it is impotent to deal with them *adequately* without taking into account the existential conditions in which such problems are embodied. And hence it must also take into consideration the *de facto* state in which human life is established (in itself and in its relations with the universe), its finalities not merely possible but really given, and therefore a host of other matters which depend on superior lights.

It should be added that even independently of this link with practical philosophy there exist many problems which metaphysics simply as a speculative science "poses but does not resolve, or resolves incompletely, and whose solution is provided by faith yet grasped in all its truth and its fitness only in the light of infused contemplation. . . . Like any human science metaphysics leaves us unsatisfied. Being turned toward the First Cause, and harboring a natural desire for knowing It perfectly, it is only natural that it should awaken in us a desire—inefficacious and conditional but real—to see this Cause in itself, to contemplate God's essence. It can never fulfil this desire."[23] So there is, as Mr. Blondel has justly observed, a void or an incompleteness of which every discerning metaphysic must necessarily become aware, and which without in any wise anticipating the nature of the answer, will find at one and the same time better fulfilment and further deepening (and this in an ever-increasing measure until God is seen face to face) in the Christian answer. But here again, owing to its state in the human soul, philosophy has need of objective illumining and of the succor of faith to attain full self-realization. Even if we are able to say that in virtue of the above-mentioned desire the true metaphysics is *naturaliter christiana,* it will as a matter of fact meet with as much difficulty in disclosing this desire in its pure form and in arriving at an exact awareness of this void as in gaining the flawless possession of the loftiest truths of reason. It is by being effectively Christian in the sense which I have tried to make clear above that it will reach this twofold objective.

Final Observations

18. I should not conceal the fact that the solution which I have proposed is tantamount to saying that in a Christian regimen philosophy enjoys improved conditions of exercise, a duly privileged state. Historical evidence of this may be found both in the extraordinary metaphysical vigor of the medieval writers, from whom —as in Leibnitz's time—it is always profitable for us to learn in these matters, and in the philosophic flowering (a strictly philosophic one, such as was not seen in the golden age of India) which the West witnessed in post-medieval times. St. Thomas himself profoundly realized the superiority of this state, when he deemed

that without the aid of revelation the philosophers would have remained in ignorance of the sublimest truths, or apprehended them only with a great deal of difficulty.[24]

But where the achievements of the intelligence are concerned, the mere question of the human being's state is hardly enough, alas; genius is also necessary. That is why Christian philosophy would make a mistake in affecting a prideful attitude; its own history during the XIV and XV centuries would suffice to counsel modesty. When we compare the genius of a Spinoza or a Hegel, not to be sure with that of St. Augustine or St. Thomas but with that of their undistinguished but well-meaning postcartesian and postkantian disciples, we are reminded of St. Jerome's comment in reference to the patriarchs and the conditions of natural law in which they lived (with particular reference to the polygamic system): Abraham was holier than I, but my state is better.

Moreover, it does not appear possible to dispense with this idea of qualitatively diverse states or conditions of exercise for philosophy. Those who do not admit that the diversity in question may stem from a certain intervention of the eternal in time and from a certain elevation of nature by the grace of a transcendent God, will have it stem from the flow of time itself, and from the succession of intellectual epochs (a succession, however, which is ideally corrected to account for regressions, those annoying regressions, which mar the historian's prescience). In this way—and taking these corrections into consideration—the privileged state follows the vagaries of the flux of time. So much so, in fact, that all that is needed to do away with any idea is simply to assign it a date of origin prior to the onset of the temporal zone thus privileged.

If I deem it inconceivable that intelligible objects are subject to an aging-process, or that a chronometric criterion suffices to evaluate our relationship with them, I believe on the other hand, that we must make room for a certain historical growth which creates—mainly as a result of the development of the positive sciences —ever new conditions of existence and exercise, an ever renewed *state* for philosophy. (Whether or not this state is a privileged one is another matter; it is, at all events, one which philosophy can reject only at the risk of becoming a mere museum piece.) I do not admit, however, that the essence of philosophy is changed on that account. And, it is my view that although Christian philosophy took form during the Middle Ages, its nature was not struck by an exclusively medieval, precopernican, precartesian, or preeinsteinian—in short prehistoric—stamp. Now that it has been freed, thanks to Galileo and Descartes, from the dead weight of that Aristotelian astronomy and pseudophysics which some still persist in confounding with its metaphysics, I believe it can take its place on the morrow (depending on its powers of assimilation) in a perfectly contemporaneous status.

19. We have stated that Christian philosophy ought not to succumb to pride. Have we laid enough stress on the privileges to which we were then alluding? Our reflections on the state and existential conditions of thought forbid that we minimize their importance. We not only stated that a Christian state exists for the philosophizing human subject, for the philosopher; whereupon we could merely conclude that there are Christian philosophers: we said that there exists a Christian state for philosophy itself, and therefore that there are not only Christian philosophers but there is a Christian philosophy as well. Philosophy is of necessity in a Christian or non-Christian state, that is to say, in the modern world and for those regions to which the New Law has been promulgated, in a Christian state or in a state fallen from Christianity, in a state of integral nature or a state of deviation. This explains the unhappy state of affairs—somewhat humiliating for the philosopher, but which it would be more humiliating still to refuse to face,—which consists in the fact that the very word philosophy has become fairly equivocal depending on whether it is used by one group or another. When certain modern idealists discuss the nature of philosophy they are talking of something almost entirely different from what we who believe in the reality of things understand by this term: an indefinable something which began to achieve self-awareness no more than three centuries ago, which has no specifying object, and which consists

ultimately in devouring and reflecting upon the findings of the physicists and the mathematicians. It is not impossible to discern at the root of this conception a vague craving to win for the human mind the plenteous self-satisfaction which Jean Jacques attributed to divinity when he expressed a wish to be "like God,"— fully content with himself and his conscience.

This is indeed a far cry from the idea of wisdom, which Christian Scholasticism for a while managed to bestow on our civilization.

For we can hardly repeat it too often: it was the Scholastic doctors who, by distinguishing in most rigorous fashion the order of knowledge from that of affectivity, by regulating their thought exclusively in accordance with the objective exigencies of being, taught Western civilization the value of truth and what speculative purity, or chastity, ought to be—a complete detachment from every biological consideration and all urging of the appetites, a sheer disinterest, even in those concerns which man holds most sacred. Is it not precisely for this too thorough speculative indifference to subjective propensities and tastes, for its too pure objectivity, that many thinkers cannot see fit to forgive Thomism? It was the devotion of the Christian era to the Incarnate Truth which enabled the intelligence to rise to the superior level of purity which was to serve science itself so well when it came to work out its own distinctive methods. The medieval intelligence was, as it were, infatuated with objectivity by the very fact that it was fixed on a superhuman object. Rationalism, through its denial of all truth above the level of reason, that is to say, by conceding reason priority over truth, has been a first and radical breach of contemplative objectivity. In our own day it is in the sphere of phenomenal science alone that a last trace of this speculative purity has been finally preserved. I have no fault to find with present-day rationalists, such as Mr. Brunschvicg, for their admiration and reverence for the intellectual ascesis of the physicist. My reproach bears rather on their failure to see therein a first step or a first inclination toward an ascesis and spirituality of the intelligence which finds its only normal goal in the loving contemplation of the saints.

It is no great accomplishment for a philosophy to be dramatic, it need only give way to its human penchants. But there are two ways for a philosophy not to be so: either not to appreciate the drama of human life, or to be too keenly aware of it. The latter, in my judgment, is the case of Thomism. It was not only at the cost of a rigorous discipline that the thought schooled in the Middle Ages learned to train its sights on the sole and immaculate truth: it was thanks as well to a distinctively Christian love of the sanctity of truth. The daring which reason evinces in scientific research betrays at its first historical inception a moment surpassing mere reason: an absolute, God-given certitude which faith affords the Christian, that by turning his regard from man to seek truth in its purity there is no danger of working against man; for God is; and the outcome is His concern; and we love Him for Himself and all else for His sake. It is because, at a certain moment of history, men knew that God was Subsisting Truth; and because they loved above all One who said: "The truth will set you free," and "I am come into the world to give testimony to the truth," and "I am the truth;" it is for all this that despite every obstacle, a religious respect for truth has—or had—developed in the heart of our culture, and that all truth even the most obscure, the most importunate, or the most dangerous, has become *sacred*, simply because it is truth.

When we declare that the Christian state of philosophy is a superior and privileged one, it is first and above all because in this state alone philosophy can fully recognize that truth is holy insofar as it is truth, and approach *holy truth* with a respect that is plenary and universal—with a respect that is so human in the highest sense of this word that its supra-human origin must be acknowledged.

REFERENCES

1. Cf. *Bulletin de la Société Française de Philosophie*, March-June 1931.

2. *The Spirit of Mediaeval Philosophy* (Scribner's: New York, 1936).

3. "Y a-t-il une Philosophie Chrétienne?" Revue de Métaphysique et de Morale (April-June, 1931). Cf. Mr. Bréhier's contribution at

the session of the *Société de Philosophie* in the Bulletin cited above.

4. "The partitioning which Mr. Bréhier applies to St. Augustine's thought with so heavy a hand, separating it into his philosophy ('that of Plato and Plotinus') and his Christian faith, gives as nothing else could the impression that this historian, whose scholarship and probity none will contest, is utterly incapable of penetrating a doctrine in which precisely those elements which his type of analysis dissociates are intimately fused. Mr. Gilson, in contrast, who communes with Augustinism from within, has made a truly remarkable effort to show how in the works of the great Doctors, and most of all perhaps in those of St. Thomas, the concepts borrowed from Greek philosophy are struck with a stamp which is radically new, and which profoundly modifies their nature. One cannot hope by a simple process of taking inventories and comparing isolated terms instead of ideas to reach that living truth which even for—and perhaps especially for—the philosopher is the only one that counts." Gabriel Marcel, *Nouvelle Revue des Jeunes,* March 15, 1932.

5. It is regrettable to see this same statement come from the pen of Mr. Michel Souriau (*Revue de Métaphysique et de Morale.* July-September, 1932, p. 365), who on Mr. Bréhier's authority presents as an accepted truth this glaring error which originated in a misinterpreted text. Are we to conclude that the Latin of the *De Unitate Intellectus* is too arduous for otherwise exacting and erudite scholars?

6. In these chapters Mr. Blondel avails himself of his friend Canon Mallet's studies on Dechamp, and cites lengthy passages therefrom.

7. This apologetics, as we know, lays stress on the inter-relation between these two facts: our fallen but virtually redeemed nature's vocation to a revelation of which it is unaware, and the presence of the Church which propounds this revelation, *tanquam potestatem habens,* and which, according to Bossuet's expression, is itself a "continuous miracle."

8. *La Crédibilité et l'Apologetique.*

9. *De Revelatione.*

10. See Note I.

11. Cf. R. Garrigou-Lagrange, *De Revelatione,* Prolegomena, Cap. 2 and 3.

12. This position, we must bear in mind, differs appreciably from that which Mr. Gilson adopted in some of his earliest works.

13. Cf. Régis Jolivet, *Essai sur les rapports entre la pensée grecque et la pensée chrétienne,* Paris, Vrin, 1931.

14. Cf. *De la Sagesse Augustinienne* (Revue de Philosophie, July-December 1930; reproduced in *Les Degrés du Savoir*); *Discours pour l'inauguration du monument au Cardinal Mercier, a Louvain (Inauguration du monument érigé au Cardinal Mercier,* pp. 44-52. Louvain, 1931); *The Dream of Descartes,* New York Philosophical Library; *Les Degrés du Savoir,* Paris, Desclée De Brouwer, 1932.

15. Cf. Ramon Fernandez, *Religion et Philosophie,* Nouvelle Revue Française, May 1, 1932.

16. *Sum. Theol.,* II-II, 45, 2.

17. "The first principle and first being." *Metaphysica,* Λ, 1073 a 23.

18. On this subject of the *Logos,* allow me to mention for the benefit of those thinkers who are fond of disaffecting the term Word (*Verbum*), and who pretend in this way "to restore to the philosophers their rightful property," Father Lagrange's studies and Father Lebreton's book, *Les Origines du Dogme de la Trinité.* Whoever would go into the question of the *Logos* cannot afford to ignore these works.

19. Gabriel Marcel, *Nouvelle Revue des Jeunes,* March 15, 1932.

20. A more precise discussion of the nature of theology will be found in Note II at the end of the book.

21. It is in this sense that for my own part I was led in works of a philosophical character (Cf. *Distinguer pour unir ou les Degrés du Savoir*) to undertake a study of the problem of mystical experience, while drawing my inspiration from St. Thomas and St. John of the Cross.

22. See Note II, p. 61.

23. *Les Degrés du Savoir,* p. 562.

24. "Ratio enim humana in rebus divinis est multum deficiens." (Human reason is very deficient in things concerning God.) *Sum. Theol.,* II-II, 2, 4. Cf. *Sum. Contra Gent.,* I, 4; *Compend. Theol.,* cap. 36; *de Verit.,* 14, 10; in *Boet. de Trin.* 3, 1, ad 3.

Notes

I

On the Nature of Apologetics

(Clarification on Mr. Blondel's Position)[1]

In this note I propose to sum up—for the most part by simply translating the Latin text itself—and to comment briefly on a few theses on the nature of apologetics advocated by Father Garrigou-Lagrange in his work *De Revelatione.*

1. As a rational defense of divine revelation, apologetics proceeds according to the natural light of reason under the positive guidance of faith.

It pertains to the *very essence* of apologetics to defend the faith *under the positive guidance of faith* itself. In other words, it must of necessity base itself not on motives of credibility discovered by our reason alone, but on those which God Himself, the Author of revelation, proposes as naturally knowable and naturally cogent signs of revelation.

2. Apologetics is positively and intrinsically under the direction of faith not only because of its state in

the human subject but also because of its very nature and its specifying object. This, of course, does not mean that its arguments would spring from faith, but that it receives from God the very concepts and the truths which it is its business to defend rationally (for example, the notions of revelation, faith, and the like), and also the kind of proofs it ought to employ in this rational defense. When God communicated to us mysteries surpassing our reason as objects of faith, at the same time He taught the way whereby their credibility best prevails upon reason, by giving us visible testimonies, especially those of miracles, prophecies and the fact of the Church, to confirm the testimonies of the invisible revelation. Thus, through the prophets, Christ, and the Apostles God Himself is Master of apologists, just as He is Master of theologians. The witnesses of Tradition have always held that the defense of the faith, as well as the exposition of the mysteries, stems from the evangelical preaching. The apologetical edifice ought not to rise from earth to heaven like a tower of Babel; like the ladder in Jacob's dream, it rests on the earth, reaching down from heaven.

3. And so it is incumbent on theology, as the supreme science, to defend its principles and therefore the faith itself against the adversaries of faith, just as it is the task of metaphysics, as supreme science of the natural order, to defend the real value of reason and of its principles against the skeptics (as Aristotle did in Book IV of the Metaphysics before treating of being

and of God as the Cause of being). In this defence of faith, theology *makes use of* purely rational knowledge and of history.

We may add that it carries out this task in conformity with its own proper mode, the speculative; and thus is set up the speculatively-practical science of apologetics (speculative in its mode, practical in its end, which is to lead souls to the faith). From this we distinguish the practically-practical science (or art) of apologetics, which is an extension of the theological *habitus* to the strictly practical domain. By virtue of its essence it calls for certain rectifications of will, already effected in the teacher, and yet to be effected in the hearer. It is to this science (or art) in particular, confirmed as it is in the teachings of speculative theology, that properly falls the task of bringing man to an awareness of his state of emptiness and anguish—a science at which Pascal above all was master. It is not this practical apologetics, however, but the speculative apologetics (speculatively-practical) which we are chiefly interested in here.

4. It should be well understood that the compelling force and efficacy of this rational defense of faith under the guidance of faith itself is properly fitted to enlighten and convince purely natural reason. Thus it is that the prophet, under the guidance of faith, proffers naturally knowable signs of the revelation made to him.

And so we must not confuse, moreover, the rational

process whereby a soul approaches faith with the rational defense of faith, with the science of apologetics, nor him who hears the evangelical or apologetical preaching with the apologist himself. The apologist, for a fact, did not make his way to the faith simply as an apologist, but indeed as a hearer of the evangelical preaching and the teaching of the Church. Only after having been firmly grounded himself in the things from above does he then, under the guidance of faith, teach the way that leads to faith and proceed to defend it. After all, one can defend only what one already has. A man enters life, for instance, inasmuch as he was engendered by his father; yet when he himself engenders in his turn, it is not inasmuch as engendered by his father that he does so, but as having now become a man. By the same token, it is not the apprentice who tutors, but the well informed. When the apostles converted the world they were not searching for the truth of faith, they had found it.

5. Otherwise stated, we may look at the proofs of apologetics, and the motives of credibility it puts to use from a twofold viewpoint: either in so far as freely proposed by God, Who has indicated them as the efficacious means of leading souls to the faith; or in so far as their efficacy and cogency is within the ambit of the unassisted reason of those to whom the apologist speaks. So what the semirationalists mistakenly affirmed of the supernatural mysteries themselves happens to be

true of the motives of credibility: they are *proposed* by God revealing, but then *proved by reason*.

6. The upshot of all this is that as a science (a specu-latively-practical science) apologetics is not specifically distinct from theology; it is merely a part or special function of theology, in fact, that part in which simply as the supreme wisdom or the supreme science theology rationally defends its own principles.

Theology, in the strict sense, by its very nature formulates its arguments in virtue of faith: from a revealed premise and a premise of reason or from two revealed premises it deduces a theological conclusion. Apologetics by nature argues in virtue of reason under the positive direction of faith, for unaided reason is in-sufficient of itself to discover motives of credibility strictly and completely proportionate to their object. Means must, in effect, be proportionate to their end; and in the present instance the end, namely, the de-fense of faith and the preparation of souls for the reception of God's gift, is of the supernatural and re-vealed order; consequently, the rational tools which such an undertaking employs in the order of discovery must of necessity derive from revelation itself, even though the task of judging of their value is the preroga-tive of reason.

It is of the nature of pure philosophy, contrariwise, to found its arguments on reason alone. And even if in fact it has need of the succor of faith and the Christian life for support in its purely rational operations, this is due to its state in the subject, and not, as in the case of apologetics, due to the exigencies of its essence.

Thus, Ollé Laprune's declaration, which Father Garrigou-Lagrange quotes in a page of his *De Revelatione,* may be applied, though not in the same sense, both to apologetics and Christian philosophy:[2] to apologetics in the sense that in the order of specification itself apologetics must be born to reason through the medium of revelation; to Christian philosophy in the sense that in the order of exercise Christian philosophy must in actual fact be fortified by revelation and instructed by it with regard to truths which in principle it *should have been able* to discover all on its own.

7. What is to be said now of the Christian philosophy of human things, or of moral philosophy adequately considered, which is discussed in an earlier part of this study and in the Note which follows? It is by virtue of the exigencies of its very object—its practical and existential object—and in order to adjust itself to this object, that it requires the lights of faith and theology. Nevertheless, it remains essentially distinct from apologetics, because, on the one hand, being subalternated to theology, considered not only in its role of rational defense of the faith but in its fullest scope, it utilizes principles issuing from the sphere of revelation; whereas apologetics proceeds by means of a purely

rational kind of proof. Then again, its object is not at
all to defend the faith or to lead souls thereto. Such
an aim may engage the philosopher—and also the
scientist or the artist—as a human being; it will never
have any interior or consubstantial link with philosophy. From which we may conclude that as a science
(a speculatively-practical science) apologetics must be
regarded exclusively as a part of theology.

It is possible for philosophical systems (even though
suffering from more or less serious defects) and above
all for that Christian philosophy of human acts, that
practical philosophy in its perfected state of which we
have spoken, to abound in precious apologetical values
and even to set forth apologetical conclusions of great
importance; these values and conclusions remain ex-
traneous to the proper task of philosophy.

II

On Moral Philosophy

(Elucidations on Moral Philosophy
Adequately Considered)[3]

1. Two objections may be raised in opposition to the
thesis I have upheld on the subject of moral philosophy
adequately considered.[4]

I. Does it not amount to a complete rejection of
all purely natural ethics?

II. Is not, in reality, what I call "practical philosophy adequately considered," or "practical philosophy subalternate to theology," theology pure and simple, not philosophy?

I should like to reply briefly to these questions.

ON NATURAL ETHICS

2. The view which I have advanced does not entail the dispossession of all purely natural ethics. It is my view that a natural morality really exists, and that its role is absolutely fundamental (as is plainly evidenced, to choose but one example, by the theory of natural virtues which an Aristotle found it possible to formulate). But this natural morality does not exist *separately* as a fully true science of conduct (any more than without charity the natural virtues exist as fully true virtues).[5] It exists merely as a structural framework of the integral moral science: a living framework, as it were, which is part of a living organism, and which is not viable—as a science of human acts sufficiently complete and *in gradu verae scientiae*—apart from this living whole. It is incapable of separate existence as a science of human conduct; it can be considered apart only if set off by way of abstraction as a part of this science and as a collection of truths which is incomplete and fragmentary, unable (if taken alone) to achieve the organic unity a science should have, and to achieve in the mind a fully and entirely correct preparation, even remote, of the act which is to be brought into concrete existence.

For this it lacks two things: the knowledge of the true ultimate end to which man is actually ordained, and the knowledge of the integral conditions of man's actual existence. Let us realize at this point that moral science is not a speculative but a practical (speculatively practical) science, from the outset turned toward the existential and toward real behavior. As a body of doctrine constituting an authentic science of human behavior, a purely natural ethic could merely be the science of conduct of man supposedly in the state of pure nature. And precisely the existential conditions which this state connotes are not, and were never given, in actual fact, but occupy the realm of simple possibility; in other words, they fall outside the province of moral science.

3. It is one thing to possess a speculative knowledge of *human nature,* to know the essence of the human being, which remains unchanged throughout the divers states of which this nature is capable (this despite the fact that in the state of fallen nature, even after having been restored by grace, it remains "wounded," weakened in its liberty and salutary forces, but given new strength by contact with other wounds, in this instance sacred); it is quite another thing to have the practical science *of the conduct of man* in the state of pure nature.

I do not think natural ethics *is* such practical science; it *would be* or *would become* such (by being organized and completed along other lines) *if* man were in the state of pure nature. In real fact, it is the ensemble (neither completely nor organically constructed even insofar as just natural) of practical truths or ethical truths which depend on the sole consideration and the sole exigencies of man's essence. It is for this reason essentially incomplete;[6] for it is not the human essence which acts, but man in the concrete, who is known as such only on condition that both his essence and his existential conditions are known.

4. There is, therefore, only one science of human conduct which is authentic, complete, and capable of existing as such *in gradu scientiae practicae:* it is that one which takes into account at once the essence and the state, the order of nature and the order of grace. All the great ethical systems which are ignorant of the ways of grace, however rich in partial truths they may be, are bound to be deficient.

What in the light of all this are we to think of Aristotle's ethics, which St. Thomas commented upon? It too is deficient. It is, if you wish, the closest approach to what the aforesaid practical science of human conduct in a state of pure nature *would be;* still it is certainly not that science any more than the rest. We should say rather that its outstanding value lies in its wealth of practical truths which stem from the sole consideration of human nature. And that is why it presents us with a great number of insights and principles from natural ethics in the sense I have defined it, that is, an *abstractly isolated* part of ethics purely and simply so-called, or again, *practical philosophy inadequately considered*. It is from this standpoint that St. Thomas commented on it. However, we gather from these remarks that his commentaries ought not to be used without discretion, and that this is not always a simple matter. For St. Thomas, steadfast in his clearly defined role of commentator, rigorously restricts himself to the literal interpretation of Aristotle's text; but true at the same time to the claims of moral science he integrates this literal explanation as far as possible— explicitly or implicitly as occasion demands—with the complete system of moral science. In view of this restriction to the letter of Aristotle, we should err in taking these commentaries on the Ethics and the Politics for a Christian moral system, or for a finished and adequate formulation of moral science (they are rather a proximate preparation therefor). And in view of the bent of the interpretations furnished, it would be equally erroneous to see in them a simple exegesis of Aristotelian ethics (they are an exegesis of Aristotle, but in a higher perspective).

ON MORAL PHILOSOPHY ADEQUATELY CONSIDERED

5. Is moral science taken in its integral sense—alone capable of standing *in gradu scientiae* as a regulative knowledge of human conduct—exclusively set up by the moral branch of theology? Or ought we to split it in two, so to speak, and distinguish, on two differing

levels of knowing, between moral theology on the one hand and a philosophical ethics subalternated to theology on the other? I have already replied no to the first of these questions and yes to the second.

Objection will doubtless be made that in such case these two sciences, one philosophic, the other theological, cover the same domain, and that both make use of the same faculty of knowing and distinguishing: *ratio fide illustrata*. Hence that which we call practical philosophy subalternated to theology[7] would in reality be nothing else but moral theology itself.

6. To these objections I reply that the domain covered by a science has either to do with its material object only, or with its formal object considered from the viewpoint of what determines the object as a thing (*ratio formalis quae*), but not from that of what determines it precisely as an object of knowledge (*ratio formalis sub qua*). Now it is on this ultra-formal determination that the specification of the sciences properly depends.

Thus, on the one hand, theodicy, or natural theology, and the theological treatise *De Deo Uno* have the same *material* object; while on the other hand the intuitive science of the blessed (the beatific vision) and theology, though differing essentially in virtue of the *ratio formalis sub qua*, have from the angle of the *ratio formalis quae* the same formal object or subject,[8] namely, God simply according to His deity (Cf. Cajetan

I, q. 1, a 2, 3, 7). For two sciences to cover the same field, therefore, by no means suffices to put both in the same species. Practical philosophy adequately considered (that is to say, truly apt to guide human action—from a distance—without error) and moral theology can cover the same field and have the same object, human acts, and still remain two specifically distinct forms of knowledge by reason of the formal determinant *sub quo.*

It should be remarked, furthermore, that the subjective faculty or means of knowing and grasping, which in both these cases is reason enlightened by faith constitutes—just as unassisted reason does in the sphere of purely natural ways of knowing—a cognitive energy of too wide a generic order to constitute the subjective correlative to the formal determinant which specifies a science. The prudence which is of the Holy Ghost, for example, likewise comes to us from reason illumined by faith, and yet in this case the subjective means of knowing, specifically considered, is the gift of counsel. In the case before us this subjective means of knowing is the theological *habitus* on the one hand and the *habitus* of moral philosophy in its perfected state on the other. And it is my contention that although the latter *habitus* is elevated through its subalternation to theology and thus ceases to be purely philosophic, nevertheless it remains by its very nature in the philosophic order.

7. If we wish to determine with greater precision why and how these two cognitive *habitus* ought to be differentiated, we can do no better than to have recourse to the explanations which Cajetan gives in I, q. 1, a. 3 and 7, and which John of St. Thomas completed in his *Curs. Theol.* I. P., q. 1 disp. 2, a. 3 to 11. In this way we can apply to the present case the general doctrine elaborated by the Thomists in connection with the case—so different in other respects—of the distinction between the beatific vision and theology, which is subalternated to it.

"Consider that in science there are two perspectives in which an object may be known: that of the *object as a thing,* and that of the *object as an object;* or again, the aspect 'which' *(quae)* and the aspect 'under which' *(sub qua).*

"The formal perspective of the *object as thing,* or *quae,* is that perspective of the reality before the mind which first receives the operations of the particular *habitus* in question, and from which the properties of this or that subject of knowledge spring, and which serves as the first means of demonstration, for example: *being* in metaphysics, *quantity* in mathematics, and *mutability* in natural philosophy.

"The formal perspective of the *object as object,* or *sub qua,* however, consists in a certain type of immateriality, or in a certain mode of abstracting and defining, for example: without all matter in metaphysics, with intelligible matter only in mathematics, and with sensible, but not individual, matter in natural philosophy . . ."[9]

Taking this point of view of the *ratio formalis sub qua,* we notice that the objects of knowledge divide "into what can be known through the light[10] of metaphysics, that is, a medium illumined by an absence of every trace of matter; through the light of mathematics, that is, a medium illumined by sensible immateriality but darkened by intelligible matter; through the physical light, or a medium obscured by sensible matter yet illumined by abstraction from individual material conditions; and through the divine light, or a medium radiating a divine effulgence. This latter constitutes theological knowledge.

". . . The unity and specific diversity of the sciences depend on the unity and diversity of the formal reasons of the objects as objects, under which *(sub quibus)* the reality is known. . . . The reason why theology is one science is to be attributed to the unity of the formal reason *sub qua,* or of the object as object, namely, *the divine light of revelation.* Everything is said to be considered in theology *insofar as divinely revealable.*

". . . There is only one adequate formal perspective of the object as object which corresponds to deity, and that is the divine light. Yet this formal perspective does not constitute a specific but a generic unity, and is divided into the divine evident light, the divine revealing light, considered apart from its evidence or inevidence, and the divine non-evident light. The first of these lights is the perspective *sub qua* of the theology of the blessed; the second, that of our theology; and the third, that of faith. And so, for the single formal reason of the object as a thing we have a specific diversity of the formal reasons of this object as an object, and consequently a specific diversity of *habitus*."[11]

Thus, in theology that which FORMALLY DETERMINES THE OBJECT AS A THING, the *ratio formalis quae,* is *deity;* and the FORMAL OBJECT, or formal subject, is God considered in His very deity, *Deus sub ratione suae propriae quidditatis* (Cajetan, *ibid.,* a. 7). Although theology has this formal reason (*ratio*) and this formal object in common with the intuitive science of the blessed, it is specifically distinct from the latter by reason of what FORMALLY DETERMINES THE OBJECT AS AN OBJECT, or the *ratio formalis sub qua,* namely, revealability as such, or *lumen divinae revelationis (abstrahendo ab evidentia et inevidentia).*

And now what is the FORMAL DETERMINANT OF THE OBJECT AS A THING, or the *ratio formalis quae* of moral philosophy, that is, of moral philosophy adequately considered or in its completed state, *in gradu verae scientiae practicae?*—It is the conformity of human liberty to its rule or its ordination toward the proper ends of human life.

What is its FORMAL OBJECT (or formal subject)?—Human acts insofar as they can be directed toward these ends, *subjectum philosophiae moralis est actio humana ordinata ad finem.*[12]

This formal object and this formal reason or view-point are common to moral philosophy adequately understood and to the moral branch of theology, because the only true last end to which man is ordained factually or existentially, and which a veritable and complete science of human behavior must envisage, is the supernatural last end. Yet just as the beatific vision and theology have the same *ratio formalis quae* but a different specifying ultimate formal perspective *(ratio formalis sub qua),* likewise moral philosophy adequately considered and moral theology differ specifically in virtue of the *ratio formalis sub qua.*

What then is this FORMAL DETERMINANT OF THE OBJECT AS OBJECT, this *ratio formalis sub qua* of moral philosophy adequately considered? Certainly it is not the divinely revealable! Rather it is *that (in human acts) which can be ordered and regulated by human reason (suitably completed).*[13] This is the ultimate formal determinant to which the proper light of a specific *habitus* corresponds, namely, the *habitus* of practical philosophy elevated and completed, *gratia materiae,* by its subalternation to theology.

8. It is manifest that there is an essential and absolutely decisive difference between this *ratio formalis sub qua* and that of theology, which is the divinely revealable. In one case we are dealing with a human and finite science that has been uplifted and completed, in the other with a certain created participation in the infinite science itself: "Science is first divided into in-

finite and finite; whereupon finite science divides into speculative and practical."[14] (CAJETAN, *ibid.*, a. 4)

In other words, in theology judgments are resolved, thanks to faith, in the light of divine revelation and finally in the increate light.[15] It is for this reason that theology enjoys an absolutely superior unity (which corresponds to the unity of divine science itself) and is at once, in a formal and eminent way, a speculative and practical science: "The light of divine revelation (stands in relation to theology) as a perspective or a mode of knowing the object, under which *(sub quo seu qua)* the revealed matter is reached by the knower; in this way it bestows a scientific unity. . . . Sacred doctrine looks for a *single common viewpoint in both speculative and practical matters,* that is, insofar as they are divinely revealed . . . because, this science *resembles God's knowledge, Who in the same act of knowing* knows Himself and His works."[16]

In moral philosophy adequately considered, on the contrary, it is in the natural light of practical reason and experience, completed by principles necessarily received—*gratia materiae*—from theology,[17] that judgments are resolved. That is why it is wholly contained in one of the parts—the practical part—of the primary division of *finite* knowledge. Since therefore the *ratio formalis sub qua* is here commensurate to the subject matter itself, that is to say, to the *agibile,* the specific unity of this moral philosophy in its fullest sense is marked out and limited by this subject matter. The

ratio formalis sub qua of theology, in contrast, transcends this same subject matter, which thereupon loses
its specifying role entirely and is drawn up into the
science which has God Himself as its subject: "The
scope of a science is determined by the faculty which
is the source of its light."[18]

Were we to refuse thus to differentiate moral philosophy adequately considered from moral theology, we
should, I believe, either be failing to form a sufficiently
elevated idea of theology, or else subjecting philosophy
to a certain violation of its inherent rights. Moral
theology, in point of fact, *is not* just a superelevated
moral philosophy; indeed it is much more than that.
And yet *there ought to be* a superelevated moral philosophy. In the first place, it is an essential requirement of
human reason that a moral philosophy be set up which
will stand as a counterpart of speculative philosophy
in the primary division of finite knowledge. Then
again, this moral philosophy would not be adequate
to its object unless it were elevated, and the necessary
and sufficient condition of this is subalternation to
theology. Hence the practical philosophy adequately
considered, the *ratio formalis sub qua* of which we
have pointed out above.

Just as grace does not suppress nature, so theology
suppresses nothing that duly belongs to philosophy.
In fact, it is not because its object actually happens to
be bound up with an order of mysteries over and above
reason that the practical branch of knowledge—one

of the two members of the primary division of finite knowledge—ought to renounce any attempt to set itself up *in gradu verae scientiae practicae* or as a practical science adequately considered,[19] and to truly regulate human action: it is simply asked to subalternate itself to the science of these mysteries for its own completion. By its own nature philosophical reason encompasses the *agibile* and scrutinizes the universe of human matters and the moral life, not only so as to discover, in the manner of natural ethics (Cf. *supra.* §§2-4), certain principles and notions which, however basically important, are insufficient in themselves for the regulation of conduct, but to *order and regulate* conduct really adequately—albeit from a distance.[20] And this becomes possible and legitimate the moment it conforms to the actual conditions of human conduct, and borrows from theology the principles requisite to this end. The theologian's arrival on the scene does not put the philosopher to flight; far from vanishing or seeking oblivion at the theologian's approach the philosopher of morals turns to him for enlightenment. Just as theology continues to exist in heaven[21] below the beatific vision, to which it is subalternated without being suppressed, similarly on earth below theology in its practical and moral function there ought to exist an adequately conceived moral philosophy subalternated to theology though not suppressed by it—an enlarged or uplifted philosophy of human acts.

And theology, to be sure, is not an enlarged or up-

lifted philosophy! Nor is moral theology in any sense
an enlarged or uplifted moral philosophy! This would
be a corruption of the concept of theology against
which the whole Thomistic teaching on the sacred
science protests. Theology is "as it were a certain im-
print [in us] of the divine science, which is one and
simple, yet encompasses all";[22] and we have seen how
Cajetan interprets this truth: the object of theological
knowledge is constituted *per lumen divinum, idest
medium divino lumine fulgens*. The *ratio formalis sub
qua* here is "the light of divine revelation;" and everything is pondered by theology "simply insofar as
divinely revealable."[23] Before finite science is in turn
divided into the speculative and the practical, science
itself divides into infinite and finite; and it is to the
first member of this division, to the infinite or uncreated science, that theology attaches by the very fact
that it is subalternated to the science of the blessed.[24]
If speculative theology and practical theology were
specifically distinct sciences and were to be regarded
as nothing more than man-made philosophy, or our
finite science in its two opposite genera of speculative
and practical, which has been uplifted by faith[25] and
assigned the revealed deposit for its subject matter,
obviously practical philosophy adequately considered
would be nothing else but moral theology itself. But
once moral theology is related to the order of the infinite or uncreated science, and practical philosophy
adequately considered is situated in the order of finite

knowledge, it is necessary, on the contrary, to regard them as essentially distinct.

It is *in so far as they are revealable* that theology weighs all truths of its own,—the laws of human action as well as the rest,[26] and without being specified by this practical object. It is specified solely by God as reached through the objective light of revelation. Moral philosophy (adequately considered), on the other hand, ponders human acts *in so far as they are capable of being regulated by human reason (suitably completed),* —and is specified and limited by this practical object. And, in fact, it is only because the existential conditions of human action are actually tied up with realities about which revelation alone can teach us with certitude that moral philosophy adequately considered must of necessity take revelation into account—and be subalternated to theology.

9. "In sacred doctrine all things are treated *under the aspect of God.* . . . All else that is reached in this sacred science are comprehended *under God;* not as parts, or species, or accidents, but as ordained in some way to Him."[27] "Sacred doctrine does not treat of God and creatures equally, but of God primarily, and of creatures only so far as they are referable to God as their beginning or end. Hence the unity of this science is not impaired."[28] And St. Thomas writes in the *Summa Contra Gentiles:*[29] "Theology is interested in creatures *inasmuch as* they reflect a certain likeness of

God, and *forasmuch as* error concerning them leads to error in divine things. And so they are looked upon in a different light by the philosopher and by the theologian.

"Human philosophy reflects on them according to what they are in themselves *(secundum quod sunt hujusmodi);* hence it divides into different parts in accordance with the different genera of things. On the other hand, the Christian faith does not look at them in this way, but to the extent that they represent the sublimity of God, and are in one way or another directed to God Himself . . . The philosopher considers in creatures those things which pertain to them by reason of their proper nature; the believer considers in creatures those things only which pertain to them insofar as they refer to God, *secundum quod sunt ad Deum relata:* for example, as created by Him, subject to Him, and so forth.

"Accordingly, whenever matters relating to creatures are considered in common by the philosopher and the believer they are elucidated by different principles. For the philosopher takes his arguments from the proper causes of things; whereas the believer argues from the First Cause, *ex prima causa* (for example, that such a matter was divinely revealed, that it concerns the glory of God, or that God's power is infinite).

"Hence these two disciplines do not proceed in the same way. For in the scientific discipline originating in philosophic reason, which considers creatures in themselves *(secundum se)*, and leads thence to the knowledge of God, the first consideration is of creatures, and the last of God. But in the scientific discipline originating in faith, which considers creatures only with respect to God *(quae creaturas nonnisi in ordinem ad Deum considerat)*, the consideration must first be of God and thereafter of creatures. And so this form of knowledge is more perfect, since it resembles more closely the knowledge of God, Who in knowing Himself beholds all else."

These texts show quite clearly that on the practical level as well there ought to be two specifically distinct kinds of scientific discipline *(doctrina):* one considering human action *secundum se,* and commensurate with it, the other viewing it only *in reference to God revealing Himself,* and fitted to this divine object alone.

It is important at this stage to be on our guard against a possible ambiguity. Clearly, human action considered *secundum se* is directed toward God as the Final End. Nevertheless, let it be well understood, the fact of moral philosophy acknowledging the ordering of human acts to God no more suffices for it to consider them *sub ratione Dei* and thereby be transformed into theology, than the fact of theodicy recognizing the creation of things by God suffices for it to consider them *sub ratione Dei* and thus be changed into theology. A purely natural ethic which directed human acts to God as natural ultimate end would not for that reason be considering human acts *sub ratione Dei.* Nor, by the same token, does moral philosophy adequately considered, which in virtue of its subalternation to theology directs human acts to man's true—and supernatural—ultimate end, consider them on that account *sub ratione Dei*. It is only when the *ratio formalis sub qua* itself is of the divine order, it is only to the extent that they are referred to God *in the formal viewpoint of revelation*, or in function of a communication made to our minds of the knowledge God has of Himself, that human acts are considered strictly *sub ratione Dei*. And it is on this ground that they are the object of moral theology.

It is on this ground also that theology is "more speculative than practical." For not only is theology "chiefly concerned with divine things rather than with human acts,"[30] but even when treating of these latter, that is to say in its practical part, it does so on account of the perfect contemplation of God, "propter Dei speculationem,"[31] and "forasmuch as by them man is ordained to this perfect knowledge, in which eternal beatitude consists."[32] Otherwise stated, it treats of them from the formal point of view of the beatific vision, taken as their goal, and in being immersed in the light of revelation, which man has been given to guide him toward this goal, and which is in itself a certain lessened communication of this sovereign knowledge. In contrast to this, moral philosophy, even though it too refers human acts to felicity (to supernatural beatitude in the case of moral philosophy adequately considered), evidently cannot be called "more speculative than practical," because it constitutes exactly that practical part of finite knowledge which stands in contradistinction to its speculative part. The fact in point here is that although it actually refers human acts to God it nevertheless does not derive its proper light from a divine *ratio sub qua*. In order to be able to view the ordination of action to the last end in a human (but elevated) light or *ratio sub qua*, and still remain adequate to its object, it suffices that it be subalternated to theology. Instead of considering human acts themselves *under the intelligible light (ratio formalis) of God's intimate life as revealed and communicated,* moral philosophy adequately considered envisages even the supernatural end itself *under the practical and human light of human acts being capable of regulation by reason (appropriately completed).*

In other words, human conduct is considered therein not *inasmuch as* it is a supernatural mystery or *inasmuch as* connected, even in its most natural character and moments, with mysteries of the uncreated life, but rather *inasmuch as* even in its most supernatural character and moments it is human and created action.

Mutatis mutandis, we may apply to moral philosophy adequately taken and to moral theology what St. Thomas wrote about the gift of knowledge *(scientia)* and the gift of wisdom: "Since man knows God through His creatures, this seems to pertain to knowledge, to which it belongs formally, rather than to wisdom, to which it belongs materially. And when, on the contrary, we judge of creatures according to things divine, this pertains to wisdom rather than to knowledge."[33] When we treat of eternal life, viewing it from below, or in the light of reasons taken from our earthly life, we are in the realm of moral philosophy rather than in that of theology—and inversely, when we form a judgment about our earthly life, regarding it from above or according to reasons drawn from eternal life, we have rather to do with theology. We might also add that theology looks on the supernatural ultimate end first and foremost as a sharing of the intimate life of God, and that moral philosophy adequately considered looks on this same ultimate end above all insofar as it brings completion to human nature.

10. It is highly interesting to note the awkward position into which moral philosophy was forced during the baroque period of Scholasticism. Even the best treatises, like the *Summa Philosophiae* of Alamannus, could be cited as evidence. The authors of these works understood, on the one hand, the need for a moral philosophy distinct from theology. But then, owing to the established Aristotelico-Christian pedagogical routine, and owing to the fact that the mind advances at a snail's pace toward an awareness of its own internal organization, they failed to bring fully to light those characteristics of a science subalternate to theology which moral philosophy must needs possess the moment it is considered truly adequate to its object and *in gradu verae scientiae practicae*.[34]

And so, in order that the course of philosophy might

be complete, they taught a so-called purely philosophic moral philosophy; and then, in order that this "philosophy" might be true, and not such as to lead minds astray instead of instructing them, they taught under this heading a sort of fragmentation of moral theology (of the *secunda pars* of the Summa, to be exact), and in doing so they cut away or covered over the vital nerve thereof (faith and revealed data) and forced it onto the plane of pure nature, while maintaining therein a material disposition and an order or method which were not philosophic but theological. An epistemological monster was the result,—the inescapable result, since they failed to recognize that moral philosophy is a science *subalternate* to theology, that is, a philosophy, but not purely philosophic.

11. A science can be subalternated to another on account of its end, its principles (only), or its subject (and its principles). Insofar as the first of these three modes of subalternation admitted by the Schoolmen does not coincide with the second or third, it is improper, and does not concern us here.[35]

In the second mode of subalternation (as to principles), a science is purely and simply (*simpliciter*) subalternated to another when it derives its principles from this other science, which discloses them to it. So that the subalternate science does not resolve its conclusions by itself (*ex se*) in naturally known or self-evident principles. Should a science perchance resolve its conclusions in principles naturally known, and yet occasionally borrow some principles from another science, it is said to be subalternate in a certain respect (*secundum quid*) to this science.

In the third mode of subalternation (as to subject) the subject or object of the subalternate science adds a difference that is accidental relative to the subject or object of the subalternate science. Thus, acoustics, a subalternate science to arithmetic, has for its subject *sounding* number; optics, a subalternate science to geometry, the *visual* line.[36]

Whenever there is subalternation as to subject there is always subalternation as to principles; but it is possible to have subalternation as to principles without subalternation as to subject. And as Cajetan (and the whole Thomistic School with him) has so forcefully pointed out, that which comprises the essential in subalternation consists in this: that a science receives its principles from another science without making them evident by its own powers: "The conclusions of a subalternating science are evident in and through their principles immediately and without the intermediary of another *habitus*; those of the subalternated science are evident in and through principles *mediately, or through the intermediary of the subalternating scientific habitus*. Herein resides the essential and natural (*per se*) difference between the subalternating and the subalternated science. Other conditions follow which cause a science to be subalternated in a particular way, not purely and simply. We may say, for example, that one science presents 'the fact that' (*quia*), another 'the reason why' (*propter quid*); or that the object of one adds an accidental and extrinsic difference to that of the other. This latter, in fact, is the condition of subalternation as to object; the former is the true condition of subalternation as to principles because of subject matter.

"By its nature, the *habitus* of the first principles of the subalternate science is the scientific *habitus* of the subalternant. The subalternate and the subalternant sciences are not necessarily distinct from the angle of the object or subject, but rather from that of the conditions of their light. This is so because the light in the subalternant science is immediately linked with self-evident principles, whereas that of the subalternate is linked thereto mediately, that is, through the intermediary of a *habitus* of another species."[37]

Thus, theology which has the same object as the intuitive science of the blessed is nonetheless subalternate to it as to its principles, which it receives from this superior science through the intermediary of faith.

We may remark that the examples which St. Thomas gives of sciences subalternated to mathematics as to subject (or object)—*musica, perspectiva, astrologia,* that is to say, acoustics, geometrical optics, and astronomy—he gives on other occasions as examples of *scientiae mediae,* formally mathematical and materially physical.[38] It is plain, as a matter of fact, that a science subalternated to another as to object is by this very fact an "intermediary science:" materially it pertains to the order or grade of the object in which it terminates (and whose proper structure requires that an accidental difference be added to the object of the subalternant science); formally it pertains to the order or grade of this subalternant science, since it considers and knows this very object which is proper to it only in so far as it connotes the object of the subalternating science, and thus is capable of falling within the formal perspective of this latter. Thus, geometrical optics, for example, is not only subalternated to geometry, but again it is itself a formally geometrical, though materially physical, science, and (by reason of the terminus of its operations) more physical than geometrical.[39]

It is not the same with sciences subalternated only as to principles. Such a subalternation is possible only where the subalternate science attains the same object as the subalternant science in a diminished light, and consequently in a different *ratio formalis sub qua* than the subalternant science. Thus the subalternate science cannot be a *scientia media* belonging formally to the same degree as the subalternant science and materially to a lower degree: of strict necessity it belongs, as to its formal reason itself, to a degree inferior to that of the subalternant science.

12. Bearing these thoughts in mind, ought we to say that moral philosophy adequately understood is a

scientia media that is formally theological and materially philosophical? No, this is not possible. To be so, it would have to be subalternated to theology on account of its subject. But it is apparent that its subject does not add any accidental difference to that of moral theology. In both instances the subject matter is the same, namely, the *agibile*: in one, it is considered from the point of view of the divine or infinite science, or as virtually revealed; in the other, from the point of view of human or finite science, or as capable of being regulated by human reason (fittingly completed).

Moral philosophy adequately considered is subalternated to theology by reason of principles only. It is not a materially philosophic and formally theological science, but a formally philosophic science subalternated to theology.

It has an essential need of subalternation to theology, because it is from theology that it obtains its idea of man's true last end, and because in the practical order ends play the role of principles. We may say, therefore, that *moral philosophy adequately considered* is subalternated *simpliciter* to theology. On the other hand, it is because of the existential conditions in which the human subject happens to be, it is *gratia materiae,* that philosophy must thus be subalternated to theology when it enters the practical realm. Hence we may say that *philosophy* is subalternated to theology *secundum quid;* I mean, of course, when it enters the practical order and is adequate to its object therein.

It is, as we have seen earlier,[40] the characteristic of a subalternate science not to resolve its conclusions in naturally known principles save *through the intermediary of* the subalternant science; so that the *habitus* of the proximate principles of the subalternate science is by its very nature the subalternant scientific *habitus*. Does this mean, then, that moral philosophy adequately considered resolves its conclusions in naturally evident first principles by the intermediary of theology, whose proper principles are supra-rational and known by faith? Or does it mean that by the medium of theology it resolves its conclusions in the supernaturally evident principles of the science of the blessed? These two sweeping assertions are equally inadmissible.

From theology, itself subalternate to the science of the blessed, moral philosophy adequately considered receives principles that are resolvable in this self same science of the blessed, and ultimately in the increate light. Yet, this is not *in order* to resolve its conclusions in the light of divine revelation, in which case it would be identified with theology. When it makes use of principles resolvable in the light of divine revelation and finally in the increate light, its own distinctive movement does not thereby strive, with the help of theology and revelation, to attach itself to the evidence which, unattainable here below, belongs to the science of the blessed. In this regard, theological truths are simply data offered to it in the same manner as the mathematical or empiriological truths it has occasion to use.

It relinquishes to theology not only the care of demonstrating these truths but also the scientific need (inefficacious here below) of finally effecting a union with the light of the intuitively perceived uncreated principles upon which these truths depend. Faith and theology are essentially and specifically *orientated* toward the beatific vision; by their very nature they seek—that which the obstacles of this life preclude—either to be eclipsed by this vision, as in the case of faith, or to keep in continuity with it, as in that of theology. Theology, in fact, strives for this continuity for the perfection of its state as a science.[41] Moral philosophy adequately considered, on the contrary, is *orientated* toward natural and terrestrial evidence; and it is in this evidence, fittingly completed, that it asks to resolve, and actually does resolve, its principles.

On the other hand, it has no need of the offices of theology, as is all too clear, to attain naturally evident first principles; it does not need theology, for example, to gain possession of these principles in the manner that optics needs geometry to enter into possession of its own principles and resolve them (not by itself but by the intermediary of geometry) in immediately known principles. Philosophy resolves its conclusions in naturally evident first principles by its own powers.

But here we are confronted by the altogether special case of a radically natural or rational science subalternated to a formally natural but radically and virtually supernatural one.[42] It is not to *enter into possession* of its principles and its proper light, but to *perfect* these principles and this light, it is on a perfective or completive basis that it has need of theology—and necessarily so given the existential conditions of its object —for resolving its conclusions in the principles—thus completed and elevated—of practical reason. The subalternant scientific *habitus* in this case is not the *habitus* itself of the proximate principles of the subalternate science, but its necessary complement.

We do not say, then, that moral philosophy adequately considered resolves its conclusions in the light of revealed principles through the intermediary of theology, nor that it needs this intermediation of theology to resolve its conclusions in the principles of natural reason. We say that it is in need of theology and of principles which can themselves be resolved in revealed principles in order to resolve its own conclusions in the suitably completed and uplifted principles of natural reason. It is a science subalternated to theology by virtue of principles, in a pure and simple way which is not, however, radical or originative but completive and perfective.

A further distinction is needful here. In a strict manner of speaking at least, it should be said that moral philosophy adequately conceived is subalternated *to theology* and not *to faith*. In point of fact, a science is subalternate to another science, not to the principles thereof; its proper and proximate principles (or in the present instance, the principles necessarily required for perfecting and completing its proper principles) are the conclusions not the principles themselves of the subalternant science. If optics were to resolve its conclusions in the very principles of geometry and in the self-evident principles of the geometrical order, it would be continuous with geometry, existing as a part of geometry itself, and not as a science subalternated to geometry. Likewise, if moral philosophy adequately considered were to resolve its conclusions in the revealed datum, and in the very principles of theology, just as they are communicated to us by faith, it would merge with theology, of which it would become a part; it would not be a science subalternated to theology.

13. The upshot of the preceding considerations is that although the theological *habitus* is, as recalled above, natural in itself—inasmuch as it is acquired by human diligence "acquiritur studio humano,"—but supernatural virtually and in its roots (*radicaliter seu originative*), moral philosophy adequately taken is, on the contrary, natural in itself and in its roots. However, by the very fact that it is subalternated to theology it is the beneficiary of a complement or fulfilment, a superelevation that is supernatural in origin. We may say that moral philosophy adequately taken is formally and radically natural, but mediately or indirectly attached to a supernatural root.

In theology, which is rooted in faith but which takes shape in our minds through the labors, through the diligence and special industry of reason, the role of principal cause is played by the light of faith, which uses the light of reason to investigate for ends all its own whatever is virtually contained in the deposit of revelation (and in particular human action viewed under this aspect). In moral philosophy adequately considered it is the light of reason which, fittingly perfected and completed, and in the role of principal cause, scrutinizes for its own ends human action considered *secundum se* and on the level of experience and history.

From which we conclude that in theological reasoning the premises of reason (and this applies likewise to the first principles of reason themselves[43]) are elevated and judged or approved by the supernatural principles of faith, and hence participate in the same formal reason as theology (which sees its object as divinely revealable); in a word, they are employed in a ministerial way by the superior light of faith.[44] In this way, the minor of reason taken under the major of faith and participating[45] in its certitude forms with it a unique *medium* or *lumen* of demonstration[46] whereby the conclusion is rationally established in virtue of the light of revelation.

But in the reasoning of moral philosophy adequately considered the union of truths of reason with those received from theology is not brought about in virtue of the light of (virtual) revelation; in which case it would give rise to a fresh theological conclusion. The moral philosopher leaves to the theologian all consideration and concern touching the possibility of resolving in the principles of faith the conclusion reached by his reasoning. For his part, he attends only to the possibility of resolving this conclusion in the fittingly completed principles of reason; and it is by virtue of the light of reason itself—completed and illumined by faith[47] but for its own benefit or as principal cause—that he resolves his conclusions in their principles. It is in this light which is superior to the light of pure philosophy and inferior to that of theology that he draws and employs the truths received from theology.

There are, thus, two ways of linking a new conclusion to an already acquired theological conclusion, since there are two ways of making use of a principle of inference. When a major premise is used *insofar as known,* it is the light of the science in virtue of which it was known that permits us to posit the conclusion. But when this major is used *only insofar as believed,* this can no longer hold true. Then it stands rather as a fact that is imposed on us than as a means of conveying evidence; and it is the proper light of the inferior science which takes the initiative toward the conclusion. Thus the truths *seen* by the blessed in the beatific vision are for the theologian principles *believed* not *seen;* and here we have the reason why the conclusions which theology draws therefrom are borne in virtue of the theological light, and not in virtue of the evidence proper to the science of the blessed.[48]

Now every subalternate science considered as such accepts *on faith* and does not *see* the principles which it receives from the subalternating science.[49]

The purely natural premises and the premises received from theology, therefore, certainly form for moral philosophy a unique *medium* of demonstration. Not that the former (the purely natural premises) are used therein as lifted up and approved by the supernatural principles of faith and as clothed by way participation with the formal viewpoint of *revelation;* on the contrary, it is the latter (the premises received from theology) which, drawn into a light inferior to their own (albeit superior to that of pure philosophy), are used as completing the principles of natural reason, and put on the specifying formal reason of moral philosophy (of how conduct can be regulated by reason). The conclusions of moral philosophy adequately considered are thus sustained in virtue of a light other than the theological; and even if materially they coincide with those of moral theology, formally and in their logical make-up they are different conclusions.

And, in fact, the moral philosopher will accordingly find his way to a host of conclusions, whose theological equivalent the theologian on his higher plane will not as much as have dreamt of discovering. (Only upon their discovery by the philosopher will he evaluate these conclusions in his own light, *qua* theologian, and set forth their formally theological equivalents.) This is so because the questions which experience puts to the moral theologian are never raised save in relation to a transcendent order, and "inasmuch as by his acts man is ordained to the vision of God, in which his beatitude consists."[50] The questions which engage the moral philosopher, on the other hand, although inevitably tied up in one way or another with the question of our ordination to the last end, are nonetheless not raised from the formal viewpoint of man's sharing in the intimacy of God's life. They are raised from the point of view of experience itself and under the formal aspect of the sundry modalities and conditions of human action which is to be brought under the rule of reason. The moral philosopher will seek to determine, for example, with Le Play, what are the conditions that an anthropological and historical study of the most exhaustive kind will permit us to correlate with the prosperity of human societies. With the "social anthropologists," he will look for a way to detect the strata of civilization, the centers and the atmosphere of expansion from which any particular cultural fact springs. Or again, to come to those very problems of the highest level which best exemplify subalternation to theology, he will try to discover what hypotheses the study of major currents of civilization like those of India and China suggests on the question of the part played in the divinely guided destinies of mankind by those communities which have remained alien to the

Judaeo-Christian revelation. If the theologian in his turn finds his way clear to take a stand on these questions from his own particular viewpoint, it will be, it is easy to see, only after the moral philosopher has raised and worked on them for his own ends, and presented them to him for consideration.

14. A cursory remark has yet to be made. Without *faith* there could no more be a moral philosophy adequately considered than there could be a theology. For unless the faith can thus be presupposed as a condition, the moral philosopher would not be justified in accepting as principles the findings of the "science of faith"; and a vital and real subalternation of moral philosophy adequately considered to theology would no longer be possible.

And yet, if it is highly desirable, it is not strictly necessary for the moral philosopher himself to possess the science of the *theologian*. If he accepts the theologian's conclusions without a comprehension of them, his own science will be in an *imperfect state,* but it will be able to exist nonetheless as a science. Still it is only when it is continuous with theology that it will be *sub statu perfecto scientiae;* just as it is only when theology itself will be continuous with the beatific[51] vision that it will enjoy the perfect state of science, even though already here below it is properly a science.[52]

On the other hand, it is clear that when we state that moral philosophy adequately considered is subalternate to theology, the word theology should not be restricted in meaning. This philosophy ought not only to be permitted to use theological conclusions concerning the last end, or this or that particular theological conclusion: as the occasion arises, it ought to be able to avail itself of the whole gamut of theological conclusions concerning the practical order, grace, the spiritual organism of the virtues and gifts, the existential conditions of man, as well as his relations with good and evil spirits.

15. Certain consequences of a methodological nature flow from the principles which we have just established, and which touch on the nature of moral philosophy adequately considered.

As St. Thomas Aquinas teaches in the passage from the *Summa Contra Gentiles* cited earlier:[53] theology proceeds *ex prima causa*, philosophy, on the contrary, proceeds *ex propriis rerum causis*. Take for example the doctrine of the ultimate end. Since in the practical order ends play the same role as principles in the speculative, this doctrine should dominate all of moral philosophy; and yet in setting out to establish it moral philosophy will follow a different method than moral theology. Let us say that if theology, conforming to the natural conditions of our intelligence, bases itself on experience so as to show what man's last end is, this is in order to rise toward this end in a direct movement,

gathering anew, as it were, from its own superior viewpoint and for its own purposes, the most essential findings on human nature which moral philosophy itself
had reaped.[54] But moral philosophy ascends to the last
end, so to speak, by a spiral movement. It first examines
inductively in their existential diversity the habits and
customs, the internal and external deportment of man,
and then it looks to the doctrine of man's ordination
toward an eternal beatitude for the explanation
(*propter quid*) of the facts (*quia*) so gathered and
analyzed, and receives from theology, to which it is
subalternated, the decisive and supremely explicative
idea of what this beatitude really consists in, as well
as the idea of the existential state of human nature in
relation to its final end.

On the other hand, being subalternated to theology,
it is not its business to take any steps on its own to
introduce the documents of Sacred Tradition; it is
enough for it to receive from theology the truths and
insights needed for elucidating its proper objects and
for the quest of their *raison d'être*. Its cognitional instruments remain essentially—though completed as
required—the data of experience and their interpretation in a rational construct; whereas the principles of
theological science are primarily the Scriptures and the
Conciliary and Patristic Tradition, and only in a
secondary and instrumental way the pronouncements
of the philosophers.

We might say in this light that theology is by nature

a "sacred" wisdom, and that moral philosophy adequately considered remains a "secular" wisdom, which owing to the claims of its practical object seeks enlightenment from the sacred wisdom.

From this it follows that since, unlike theology, it is not obliged to proffer only what can be linked to the revealed deposit, it will concede, as we have already remarked, a *larger* role to hypothesis, induction, and constructions of an interpretative kind, and will be empowered to tackle more readily manifold problems of a secular character. In particular, it would seem that there should open before it a boundless horizon of problems which bear on the philosophy of culture, and more generally on meaning and value, the destiny and governance of the works of man, not only in relation to eternity but in relation to the created and temporal order itself and to the history of creation. Then, as though by compensation, there are other problems, particularly those wherein the mind explores the sacred depths of the revealed deposit, which will not come within the purview of moral philosophy, even adequately considered.

Let me draw attention, in the last place, to another consequence of the principles advocated here. If there were not a moral philosophy adequately considered really distinct from moral theology, then we should have to say, in any exact use of terms, that those fields of research such as the history of religion, anthropology, politics, economics, and the rest, which depend on history or on methods of positive enquiry for all the observational material they amass, and for their empirical basis—are not constituted as completely and genuinely explicative "sciences" unless integrated with theology. Only a theological anthropology or a political theology would merit the name of ethical *science* or political *science* strictly speaking. If, however, the distinction made in the course of this essay is admitted, it must be averred that these disciplines can also be set up as completely and genuinely explicative sciences (in the practical or moral realm) through integration with moral philosophy. As there ought to be a theological anthropology and a political theology, so too there ought to be a philosophic anthropology and a political philosophy in which the difference of outlook which sets off moral philosophy adequately understood from moral theology can be found, and which are by equal title and in the strict sense an anthropological *science* and a political *science* (subalternated to theology). Actually, is it not merely due to a rationalist and positivist bias—yet doubtless also because of a sense of certain properties and propensities of their *habitus*— that anthropologists, sociologists, and the like, are loath to admit that the field of their choice could attain the status of a completely and genuinely explicative science only by a theological principle. Indeed it is difficult enough to convince many of them that for this at least a philosophic ground is needful.

If asked to give an illustration of the distinction

which I am making here between political theology and political philosophy, I would say that the *De Regimine Principum* stems from the first, and that St. Thomas' Commentary on Aristotle's Politics stems from the second.[55]

These considerations are applicable to what we know today as the philosophy of religion; they show that although the "philosophy of religion" *par excellence* is theology, there is nonetheless room for a philosophic discipline in the shape of an authentic philosophy of religion. If it is to become a true science, however, it must be integrated with moral philosophy adequately considered, and hence be subalternated to theology.

REFERENCES

1. See p. 7.
2. "Intellectual integrity obliges us to own to whatever is of Christian provenance in our preoccupations, in our very questions, in our investigations, in our philosophic theories. . . . Such a solution as I have proposed derives from positive religion; but in a sense this solution was thoroughly philosophic, since it was accepted by reason and proved rationally. And yet, reason left to itself would not have discovered it. . . . That is not all. There are questions which, we must admit, reason alone would not have posed, would not have surmised. . . . Yes, in those very researches in which to the best of my ability I have used my intelligence, methodically and in accord with the laws of reason, I have often benefited from a light that is by no means a natural one." (*Le Prix de la Vie*, p. 345-347.)
3. See p. 38.
4. *ibid.*
5. Without charity a man can have, for example, not only the false temperance of the miser (specified by the *bonum utile*), but true

acquired natural temperance (specified by the *bonum honestum* in such matter). Nevertheless, without charity this true temperance remains in the state of disposition (*facile mobilis*), and does not attain the state of virtue properly so-called (*difficile mobilis*); in other words it is not fully true virtue.

6. Below the infused theological and cardinal virtues, for example, are the acquired cardinal virtues with a naturally knowable formal object and rule. Thus, acquired natural prudence proceeds by the light of the principles of natural reason, i.e., practical principles which are known by synderesis, such as: we must do good and avoid evil, we must be just, and so on.

However, as I already pointed out in the preceding note, without charity this natural acquired prudence and other cardinal virtues can exist only as dispositions and not as virtues strictly speaking. As a result, without charity they do not achieve a mutual connection, nor become bound in a single, strong organism, for such a connection is achieved only *in statu virtutis*. (Cf. St. Thomas and his commentators on this subject.) So the purely philosophic knowledge of these virtues remains something partial relative to moral science taken in its fullest sense, and is impotent to form by its own powers a complete and organically coherent doctrine of the virtues and of conduct.

7. The various modes of subalternation of one science to another will be examined later (p. 82 ff.). Then it will be seen (p. 89) that moral philosophy adequately understood ought to be considered as subalternated to theology on account of principles, and in a *pure and simple* way, which, however, is *not radical or originative* but *completive and perfective.*

8. These two words, which strictly speaking designate different things, may be used interchangeably here (Cf. John of St. Thomas, *Curs. Theol.,* I. P., q. I, disp. 2, a. 11).

9. "Nota duplicem esse rationem objecti in scientia, altera *objecti ut res*, altera *objecti ut objectum:* vel alterat ut *quae,* altera ut *sub qua.*

"Ratio formalis *objecti ut res,* seu *quae,* est ratio rei objectae, quae primo terminat actum illius habitus, et ex qua fluunt passiones illius subjecti, et quae est medium in prima demonstratione, ut *entitas* in metaphysica, *quantitas* in mathematica, et *mobilitas* in naturali.

"Ratio autem formalis *objecti ut objectum,* vel *sub qua,* est immaterialitas talis, seu talis modus abstrahendi et definiendi: puta sine omni materia in metaphysica, cum materia intelligibili tantum in

mathematica, et cum materia sensibili, non tamen hac, in naturali
. . ." (CAJETAN, in I, 1, 3).

10. The word 'light' (*lumen*) should be understood here as related
to the object and not to the way of knowing or the *habitus*. Cf. John
of St. Thomas, *Curs. Theol.*, I. P., q. 1, disp. 2, a. 7, Solesmes, I, p.
379 b.

11. ". . . in scibile per lumen metaphysicale, idest medium
illustratum per abstractionem ab omni materia; et per lumen
mathematicum, idest medium illustratum immaterialitate sensibili,
obumbratum tamen materia intelligibili; et per lumen physicum,
idest, medium obumbratum materia sensibili, illustratum autem ex
separatione individualium conditionum; et per lumen divinum, idest
medium divino lumine fulgens: quod scibile theologicum constituit.

". . . Unitas et diversitas specifica scientiarum attenduntur penes
unitatem et diversitatem rationum formalium objectorum ut objecta
sunt, vel, quod idem est, rationum formalium sub quibus res sciuntur.
Ratio quare theologia sit una scientia assignatur ex unitate rationis
formalis sub qua, seu objecti ut objectum est, idest, *luminis divinae
revelationis*. Omnia enim dicuntur considerari in theologia, *inquantum sunt divinitus revelabilia*.

". . . Deitati respondet una tantum ratio formalis adaequata
objecti, ut objectum est, et haec est lumen divinum. Sed illa ratio
formalis non est una in specie, sed in genere: et dividitur in lumen
divinum evidens, et lumen divinum revelans, abstrahendo ab evidentia et inevidentia, et lumen divinum inevidens: et primum est
ratio sub qua theologiae beatorum, secundum nostrae, tertium fidei.
Et propterea, cum unitate rationis formalis objecti, ut res, stat
diversitas specifica rationum formalium illius, ut objectum; et con-
sequenter diversitas specifica habituum." (CAJETAN, *ibid.*)

12. Otherwise stated, *actiones humanae secundum quod sunt
ordinatae ad invicem et ad finem, seu homo prout est voluntarie
agens propter finem* (human acts insofar as they are ordered among
themselves and toward their end, or man to the extent that he
voluntarily acts for an end). Alamannus, *Ethic*, q. 1, a. 1.

For his part, Goudin writes: "Objectum materiale Moralis sunt
affectus, seu actus humani; formale vero est moralitas, cujus tales
actus seu affectus aunt capaces; ratio vero sub qua, sunt prima
principia practica." (The material object of Moral Science is human
dispositions or human acts; but the formal object is the morality of
which these dispositions or acts are capable; and the formal reason
'under which' is the first practical principles.) *Ethic.*, q. praeamb., a. 1.

13. This is doubtless the meaning underlying Lesson I of St.

Thomas' Commentary on Book I of the Ethics: "Sapientis est ordinare . . . *Secundum autem diversus ordines* quos proprie ratio considerat, sunt diversae scientiae. . . . Ordo autem actionum voluntarium pertinet ad considerationem moralis philosophiae." (It is the office of the wise man to direct. . . . Furthermore, the different sciences correspond to the different orders considered by reason. . . . The order of voluntary action, moreover, belongs to the considerations of moral philosophy.) It does not suffice to say with Goudin (Cf. foregoing note) that the *ratio sub qua* of moral philosophy *sunt prima principia practica.* Strictly speaking, it is *ordinabilitas (actionum voluntarium) a ratione practica.*

14. "Scientia prius dividitur in scientiam infinitam et finitam: et deinde scientia finita dividitur in speculativam et practicam."

15. ". . . Accipit haec scientia . . . immediate a Deo per revelationem." (This science receives [its principles] . . . immediately from God through revelation.) *Sum. Theol.,* I, 1, 5, ad 2.

16. "Lumen divinae revelationis (comparatur ad theologiam) ut ratio seu modus cognoscendi objecti, sub quo seu qua attingatur res revelata a cognoscente: et sic dat unitatem scientiae. . . . Sacra doctrina attendit *unam rationem communem speculabilibus et operabilibus: scilicet inquantum sunt divinitus revelabilia* . . . quia hujusmodi scientia est *sicut scientia Dei, qui scientia eadem* scit se et opera sua." (Cajetan, *ibid.,* a. 4).

17. See below §12.

18. "Juxta facultatem luminis est extensio scientiae." Cajetan, *ibid.,* a. 7.

19. "Adequately considered" here refers to this practical science in its own order and obviously not in the sense that this practical science is expected like moral theology to put together a treatise on the theological and moral infused virtues. As a science subalternate to theology it seeks enlightenment and receives conclusions from such a treatise; it does not institute one.

20. It is prudence which regulates conduct from close at hand.

21. Cf. John of St. Thomas, *Curs. Theol.,* I. P., q. 1, a. 5, Solesmes, I, p. 365 ff.

22. ". . . velut quaedam impressio divinae scientiae, quae est una et simplex omnium." *Sum. Theol.* I, 1, 3 ad 2.

23. See above p. 69.

24. See above p. 71.

25. The fact is that in such case it would not be uplifted by faith at all, but rather the contents of faith would be submitted to the light

of philosophy; for faith would then merely supply the revealed data, while natural reason was allotted the task of seeking out their mutual relations and pondering their meaning. Theology would accordingly amount to no more than *an application of philosophy* to the revealed datum. The mere fact that dogmas should fall under the glance of the philosopher would be all that is necessary for the making of theology (Cf. my *Dream of Descartes,* ch. III). The reality of the matter is that theology is a *habitus* of wisdom which itself is *rooted in faith* and hence *supernatural,* at least in the radical and virtual sense; a *habitus* which uses philosophic knowledge instrumentally and evaluates it in its own light. A philosophical form of knowledge cannot be elevated by faith in the order of specification itself, unless it is *subalternated to a theological science which is—as in actual fact—a created participation of the divine science.*

26. ". . . Theologia procedit ex principiis revelatis in Scriptura. Sed constat in Scriptura contineri multa pertinentia ad praecepta moralia et instructionem nostram; unde dicitur (II ad Tim., III, 16, 17): *Omnis scriptura divinitus inspirata utilis est ad docendum, ad arguendum, ad corripiendum, ad erudiendum in justitia, ut perfectus sit homo Dei, ad omne opus bonum instructus.* Ergo independenter a philosophia morali, ex suis principiis revelatis potest theologia discurrere circa res morales . . ." (Theology proceeds from principles revealed in Scripture. But it is obvious that Scripture contains many things pertaining to moral precepts and to our instruction; wherefore, it is written [II Tim. III, 16, 17]: *All Scripture is inspired by God, and useful for teaching, for reproving, for correcting, for instructing in justice, that the man of God may be perfect, equipped for every good work.* Therefore, independently of moral philosophy, theology in virtue of its own revealed principles can discuss moral matters.) JOHN OF ST. THOMAS, *Curs. Theol.,* I.P., q. 1, disp. 2, a. 7, Solesmes, I, p. 377 a.

27. "Omnia pertractantur in sacra doctrina *sub ratione Dei* . . . Omnia alia quae determinantur in sacra doctrina, comprehenduntur *sub Deo:* non ut partes, vel species, vel accidentia, sed ut ordinata aliqualitur ad ipsum." *Sum. Theol.,* I, 1, 7, c. and ad 2.

28. "Sacra doctrina non determinat de Deo et de creaturis ex aequo, sed de Deo principaliter, et de creaturis *secundum quod referuntur* ad Deum, ut ad principium vel ad finem. Unde unitas scientiae non impeditur." *Ibid.,* I, 1, 3, ad 1.

29. *Sum Contra Gent.,* II, 4.

30. *Sum. Theol.* I, 1, 4.

31. Cajetan, *ibid.*

32. *Sum. Theol., ibid.*

33. "Cum homo per res creatas Deum cognoscit, magis videtur hoc pertinere ad scientiam, ad quam pertinet formaliter, quam ad sapientiam, ad quam pertinet materialiter. Et e converso, cum secundum res divinas judicamus de rebus creatis, magis hoc ad sapientiam quam ad scientiam pertinet." *Sum Theol.* II-II, 9, 2, ad 3.

34. One wonders whether Javelli (Cf. his exposition *De celsitudine divinae et christianae philosophiae moralis* in his *Christiana Philosophia,* 1640) had not sensed the problem. At all events, he did not make the explicit distinctions requisite in this matter, and thus inevitably ran the risk of confusing in practice "Christian moral philosophy" and theology. See M. D. Chenu's article *Javelli* in the *Dict. de Théol. Catholique,* V. VIII; also E. Gilson's *L'Esprit de la Philosophie Médiévale,* v. II, p. 279.

35. This first mode of subalternation may imply subalternation by reason of principles or of subject, in which case it merges with the second or third modes; (thus we say—p. 86 f.—that moral philosophy adequately considered is subalternated to theology by reason of principles, because in fact the last end of man is supernatural, and in the order of practical knowledge ends play the role of principles). Or again, it may simply mean a dependence as to use *(ministerium et imperium),*—for example, the *art* of bridlemaking is subordinated to the equestrian *art,* this latter to the military *art,* and this latter to the political *art,*—without any concern about a dependence as to *the manifestation of truth;* wherefore the subalternation (which involves the subordination of one *science* to another) is improper. Cf. John of St. Thomas, *Log.* II. P., q. 26, a. 2.

36. John of St. Thomas, *Log.,* II. P., q. 26, a. 2.

37. "Subalternantis scientiae conclusiones visibiles sunt ex et in principiis immediate, absque alio medio habitu; subalternatae vero conclusiones visibiles sunt ex et in principiis per se notis *mediate, mediante scilicet habitu scientifico subalternante;* et haec est essentialis et per se differentia inter subalternantem et subalternatam scientiam. Caeterae autem conditiones sunt consequentes, aut sunt talis subalternatae, non subalternatae ut sic. Puta, quod una dicat quia, et altera propter quid; aut quod objectum addat differentiam accidentalem et extraneam. Haec namque est conditio subalternationis quoad objectum, illa vera subalternationis quoad principia gratia materiae.

". . . Per se habitus principiorum proximorum scientiae subalternatae est habitus scientificus subalternans. Scientia subalternans et subalternata non necessario opponuntur ex parte objecti nec ex parte subjecti, sed potius ex parte conditionum medii: quia scilicet medium in subalternante immediate jungitur principiis per se notis, subalternatae vero mediate, mediante scilicet habitu alterius speciei." (CAJETAN, in I, 1, 2.) Cf. JOHN OF SAINT THOMAS, *Curs. Theol.* I. P., q. 1, disp. 2, a. 5.

38. Cf. Saint Thomas, *Sum. Theol.*, I, 1, 2; II-II, 9, 2, ad 3; in *Phys.*, lib. II, 1, 3; in *Boet. de Trin.*, 5, 1, ad 5; 5, 3, ad 6. See also my *Réflexions sur l'Intelligence*, p. 286 and *Les Degrés du Savoir*, p. 84.

39. Cf. *Les Degrés du Savoir*, pp. 84-85 and 120-125.

40. See the quotation from Cajetan, p. 83 f.

41. "Motivum ejus (sc. theologiae) non est pure naturale, sed originative et radicaliter supernaturale; et ideo continuabilis est cum lumine supernaturali claro, *et in illud inclinat ex natura sua*, secundum quod ex natura sua petit principia supernaturalia, sive fidei in via, sive luminis gloriae in patria." JOHN OF ST. THOMAS, *Curs. Theol.*, I.P., q. 1, disp. 2, a. 5. Solesmes, I, p. 368 a.

". . . Illa scientia (sc. subalternata) ex natura sua postulat continuari cum scientia subalternante." *Ibid.*, a. 3. (I, p. 354).

"Fides importat motum quemdam intellectus ad visionem in qua quietatur, fides requirit visionem gloriae, tanquam terminus status viae." *Ibid.*, II-II, q. 1, disp. 2, a. 1 (Vives, VII, p. 28-29).

(The motivating force of theology is not purely natural, but supernatural in its origin and roots. Hence it is continuous with the clear supernatural light, and *by its very nature tends toward it*, to the extent that by its nature it seeks supernatural principles, whether of faith in this life, or of the light of glory in the next.)

(. . . The subalternate science by its very nature requires to be continuous with the subalternant science.)

(Faith introduces a certain movement of the intellect toward that vision in which it finds rest; faith requires the vision of glory as the term of its earthly state.)

42. Concerning this feature of theology, cf. JOHN OF SAINT THOMAS, *Curs. Theol.*, *loc. cit.*, a. 8 and 9.

43. Cf. JOHN OF SAINT THOMAS, *Curs. Theol.* I.P., q. 1, disp. 2, a. 6 and 9, Solesmes, t. I, pp. 372b and 392b.

44. *Ibid.*, disp. 2, a. 6, Solesmes, I, p. 371a.

45. In an extrinsic way; cf. JOHN OF SAINT THOMAS, *ibid.* disp. 2, a. 7, n. 22, Solesmes, I, p. 382a.

46. *Ibid.*, a. 6, p. 372a; a. 7, pp. 377 and 381b: "Non potest praemissa naturalis componere unum medium cum praemissa de

fide, nisi per hoc quod illi subordinatur et ab ea corrigitur et judicatur, utpote a superiori a qua praemissa naturalis certitudinem suam regulat: et praemissa sic conjuncta praemissae superiori de fide, influit simul cum ipsa: non diversa ratione nec diverso lumine, sed inquantum de ejus lumine et certitudine participat; et sic constituitur una ratio formalis quae dicit virtualem revelationem et mediatam, sub qua eodem modo influit praemissa de fide, et naturalis ut elevata ab illa." (A natural premise cannot form a unified medium with the premise of faith except on condition that it be subordinated to the latter and approved and judged by it, as by a superior premise upon which the lower (natural) premise bases its certitude. Further, the natural premise thus linked to the superior premise of faith then proceeds in unity with this latter: not according to a different perspective or a different light, but inasmuch as it participates in the light and certitude of the premise of faith. And thus is established a single formal reason, which is that of virtual and mediate revelation, in virtue of which the premise of faith and the elevated natural premise proceed in the same way.)

47. Here again the first principles of reason are superelevated—not of course in such wise as to assume by way of participation the formal reason of the *revealable* (as occurs in theology due to their connection with the principles of faith), but as used, approved, and confirmed by a science which is itself subalternate to the science of the blessed.

48. Cf. JOHN OF SAINT THOMAS, *loc. cit.*, a. 5.

49. *St. Thomas Aquinas, Sum. Theol.*, I, 1, 2: "Sicut musica credit principia tradita sibi ab Arithmetico, ita doctrina sacra credit principia revelata sibi a Deo." (Just as music accepts on faith the principles taught by the arithmetician, so the sacred science accepts the principles revealed by God.) Such is also the case even when the subalternate and subalternant sciences are continuous in the same human subject. Then the intelligence sees the conclusions of the subalternant science, but with the very *habitus* of this science. The subalternant science *sees* these conclusions, which are the principles of the subalternate science, while this latter, considered as such, *believes* them (if it saw them it would become confounded with the subalternant science).

50. *Sum. Theol.* I, 1, 4.

51. Cf. JOHN OF SAINT THOMAS, *loc. cit.*, a. 5, n. 12 ff.

52. *Ibid.*, a. 3, n. 12, Solesmes, I, p. 356a.

53. *Sum. Contra Gent.*, II, 4; *Vide supra.* p. 76-78.

54. St. Thomas proceeds in this way at the beginning of the *Prima*

Secundae, just as at the beginning of the *Prima Pars* he gathers the marrow of the knowledge about nature which speculative philosophy has provided and rises by a direct movement to the First Cause. Thus, like philosophy theology employs the analytico-synthetic method, yet it does so in a different and superior manner which is not suited to philosophy. The latter must creep and linger longer among the *peculiar conditions and the created causes of things,* which provide it with appropriate means of moving forward.

55. St. Thomas' Commentaries on the Ethics and the Politics relate to moral philosophy, not to theology. They relate also to moral philosophy adequately considered; yet, in keeping with the remarks made earlier (p. 64 f.), they relate thereto rather as a step toward it, and merely as a *preparation* for an adequate practical form of knowledge.

Agibile: Literally, the doable, whatever can take the form of human action; or simply, human acts.

Analytico-Synthetic: Pertaining to the method which combines the analytic and the synthetic. The analytic method, which predominates in the natural sciences and is inductive, proceeds from the observation of facts to the formulation of the laws governing them; the synthetic method, which is dominant in speculative science and is deductive, goes from the general to the particular, from first principles to specific applications, from the simple to the complex.

Causality: In modern usage, the relationship or category of cause and effect; in Scholasticism, the quality or order of being according to which a thing depends on something else for its being or becoming. *Material causality* pertains to the undetermined or unspecified material from which the thing is constituted; *formal causality,* to the intrinsic principle or form that specifies or differentiates this material as a particular thing.

De Deo Uno: Concerning the One God: a treatise in

dogmatic theology which deals with the existence and the nature of God.

Ex prima causa: From the First Cause, that is, from God considered as Cause of all other causes.

Ex propriis rerum causis: From the proper causes of things; that is to say, from the second or created causes which constitute things. These causes from which philosophy starts are proximate and second only relative to the First Cause, God; in another sense, philosophy considers things in their first and highest causes in contradistinction to the natural sciences which deal in secondary and proximate causes.

Gratia materiae: By reason of the subject matter.

Gratia sanans: A healing or medicinal grace. One of the effects of divine grace is the health (*sanatio*) of the soul.

Habitus: A stable or habitual intellectual disposition, or let us say light, which aids or conditions the act of knowledge in attaining its object.

Hypostasierung (Ger.): An agency for giving substance to; personification (pejoratively here).

In gradu (verae) scientiae (practicae): On the level of a (true) (practical) science. (See Science)

In statu virtutis: In the state or condition of virtue; as a virtue.

Inform: To give an inner form or shape to.

Infused: Used in theology to specify virtues and gifts which have been imparted to the soul by God gratuitously, independently of human effort or merit; hence antonymous to *acquired*.

Logos (Gr.): A term which in the earlier Greek writers signified the principle of reason or intelligibility, and which later came to mean 'word'—with a cosmic connotation in either case. It is found chiefly in Heraclitus, the Stoics, and Philo, and was appropriated by St. John (Cf. Prologue of 4th Gospel), who referred it to Christ, as the Word uttered eternally by the Father, through Whom everything is made and all men are enlightened.

Motives of credibility: A phrase commonly employed by theologians and apologists to designate the signs or proofs of divine revelation, which are principally miracles, prophecies, and the marks and attributes of the Church.

Naturaliter christiana: Naturally or inherently Christian. This expression was first used by Tertullian who applied it to the soul (*anima*). It is used today to describe a philosophy which in addition to expounding the highest truths of reason, discovers by its own methods or exemplifies in itself the inner dynamism which leads to God as the final fulfillment of all things.

Object: That to which an act of knowledge is directed and in which it terminates. In criteriology this term is opposed to 'subject,' but can sometimes be synonymous with it. (See Subject.) The *material* object is that of which no specific aspect has been determined for consideration; the *formal* object is the material object considered under a specific or special point of view; the *proper* object is the one to which the act of knowledge naturally tends, and in which it is completed.

Opus rationis: Literally, the work of reason, that is to say, the philosophic effort. With *perfectum* it is used by St. Thomas to define philosophy as the perfect accomplishment of reason.

Order: In this study, a fundamental class of being; synonymous with 'sphere,' 'level,' or 'plane.'

Philosophia ancilla theologia: Philosophy the handmaid of theology.

Ratio fide illustrata: Reason enlightened by faith.

Reason (*ratio*): In psychology, the discursive faculty of the mind; in metaphysics, the essence or form of a thing; in logic (with *formal*), the light in which an object is viewed and by which it is specified. In this last sense—which is the most frequent sense used in this study—it is used interchangeably with 'aspect,' 'viewpoint,' 'perspective,' etc.

Reduplicative ut sic: In logic, a proposition is taken

reduplicatively when by means of "redoubling" phrases (as such, insofar as, as, etc.) it focuses on the formal reason of the subject, in order to consider it in itself.

Science: In its widest meaning, synonymous with knowledge; in the narrow sense, a particular discipline with its own proper object and formal reason; more precisely, an organically constituted body of evident, certain, and necessary truths. A science is *true* if it is adequate to its object and can resolve its conclusions in evident principles.

Separated Philosophy: A philosophy which claims absolute sovereignty for itself by shunning all higher wisdom and lights; any form of pure rationalism. This philosophy may be seen as stemming from Descartes who based all science on pure reason, and made science and faith mutually exclusive disciplines.

Serva: Bond-servant, slave.

Subalternation: This term signifies more than simple 'subordination' or 'infraposition,' in which cases the lower science retains its proper autonomy when employed instrumentally by the superior science: it refers rather to the state of the science which cannot exist as a true science unless it receives illumination from the higher science. Thus, the *sub-*

alternating (or subalternant) science makes its own first principles in order to become adequate to its *alternated* (or subalternate) science must take the conclusions of the subalternating science as its own first principle in order to become adequate to its object.

Subject: When this term does not designate the individual knower (psychological sense) or that of which something is predicated (in logic) it denotes (as is most frequently the case in this study) that upon which a faculty or science acts, and is synonymous with 'object.'

Synderesis: In St. Thomas, a stable inborn disposition of the intellect, or *habitus,* which inclines us to know the first principles of practical reason.

Wisdom: Knowledge through the highest sources and causes. In its highest reaches *science* coincides with wisdom, but becomes an imperfect form of it as it approaches the particular or the empirical.

Veluti stella rectrix: As a guiding star, that is to say, as an exterior and superior orientation.

INDEX OF PROPER NAMES

115